ROLLING HO...
Shelter on Wheels

Lloyd Kahn

Shelter Publications, Inc.
Bolinas, California

ROLLING HOMES
Shelter on Wheels

Lloyd Kahn

Distributed in the United States by Publishers Group West
and in Canada by Publishers Group Canada

Library of Congress Control Number: 2022934938

Names: Kahn, Lloyd, 1935– author.
Title: Rolling homes / Lloyd Kahn.
Description: Bolinas, California : Shelter Publications, 2022. |
    Series: The Shelter Library of Building Books ; 9
Identifiers:
    ISBN 9780936070896 (paperback) |
    ISBN 9780936070902 (Epub) |
    ISBN 9780936070919 (Kindle)
BISAC: HOM022000, HOM004000, HOM023000, TRA001030, PHO023090, TRV001000.
Keywords: house bus; camper van; tiny house on wheels; tiny home on wheels; house truck;
pickup with camper; gypsy wagon; vardo; trailer; van; road rig; recreational vehicle; RV;
tiny house; tiny home.

3 2 1 — 24 23 22
(Lowest digits indicate number and year of latest printing.)

Printed and bound in China

Shelter Publications, Inc.
P.O. Box 279
Bolinas, California 94924
415-868-0280

Email: shelter@shelterpub.com
Orders, toll-free: 1-800-307-0131

Lloyd's Blog: ***www.lloydkahn.com***
instagram.com/lloyd.kahn
instagram.com/shelterpub
twitter.com/lloydkahn
Shelter's Website: ***www.shelterpub.com***

Shelter
Publications

Cover photo: Erik J. Howes (see pp. 56–59)
Van drawing on opposite page: Al Ortiz Jr., © 2020 (Instagram: @alortizjr)

Contents

Vans

All-Terrain Vehicles & Cars

Solar-Powered Vehicles

Pickups with Campers

House Trucks

House Buses

Trailers

Cycles

Introduction

THERE'S A NOMADIC REVOLUTION going on these days. In the last few years, either for reasons of practicality (high costs of rent or mortgages), change in lifestyle, or the search for adventure, people are customizing all sorts of vehicles for travel.

The last decade has been an era of innovation, improved design, and, due to social media, communication of nomadic experimentation.

Mercedes Sprinter vans (along with Ford Transit vans and other high-top vehicles) have prompted a wave of rolling homes.

Advances in stoves, refrigerators, solar power, pop-tops, rooftop tents, and adaptation of many nautical devices have expanded the options for outfitting rolling homes.

This book focuses on do-it-yourself vehicles, with most of them fitted out for the road by their owners — similar to the way that Shelter's books on building feature handbuilt homes.

Of the 75 homes covered here, 29 are full-time residences. (Eleven of the vehicles are from builders who have been featured in previous Shelter books.)

You can read the stories here as if you are traveling along — riding shotgun — with the contributors: sharing their experiences. And if you're considering building a nomadic home, you'll find practical information and a wide variety of solutions honed by experience.

Included here are vans, sedans, trucks, buses, and trailers, with an extensive array of designs and styles. A number of the units are 4-wheel drive for off-road travel.

If you thumb through these pages and look at the sections on "Vital Statistics," you'll find a wealth of components to choose from if you're building a home on wheels.

There are dozens of floor plans, all sorts of sleeping arrangements, and some unique "stealth vehicles" — designed to be under the radar, so that passers-by have no idea that someone is sleeping in a parked vehicle.

There is a European mini-van designed and outfitted by a young German woman who just graduated from architectural school and took a sabbatical to go surfing. There are a number of camper truck shells, all completely different. A converted school bus that is used in both cold weather for skiing, and in warm climates (such as Baja California) for surfing.

There's a converted horse trailer furnished with Victorian antiques, which is used at Burning Man. A tiny Geo Metro (3-cylinder sedan) that is ingeniously designed for sleeping, cooking, and eating in the stealth mode. Two solar-powered electric vehicles that charge their batteries with onboard solar panels. Two travelers who criss-crossed the U.S.A. for 6,500 miles on electric-powered unicycles.

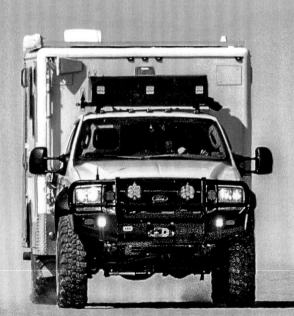

There is a wide price range. One of these units cost about $200,000. Yet most are far more modest in means, such as a homemade $300 pickup truck camper shell.

In a sense, this is a scrapbook. Most of the articles consist of stories and statistics, as well as photos sent in by Shelter's network (built up over 50 years) of hands-on people. We've got a unique collection of vehicles here because we have a network of *builders*.

It's not a book that was designed in advance, but rather an unplanned and serendipitous collection from people in different parts of the world, almost all of whom believe in using their own hands to create their own shelters. In a way, the book created its own form, based on input received. It's taken us about a year to get all this together.

Now that it's finished, it's apparent that there are two categories not present in these pages:

1. *Vanlife,* as it has come to signify: where the focus is on lifestyle, not building or creating. A young couple, who often generate income by posting their daily activiies — influencers. It's OK, as far as I'm concerned, as their alternatives are high rentals or getting locked into a bank for 30 years. The influencers probably have a lighter planetary impact than urban renters or homeowners.

2. Nomadlanders, mostly retired people who are "houseless, not homeless," per the book and the movie *Nomadland*. People who have opted for a $20,000 van as opposed to a $500,000 house. Working at Amazon, the post office during Christmas, as park rangers or fry cooks, parking in Walmart parking lots or campgrounds. A very large group of rolling homes people, but they just didn't contact us. A lot of them may want to stay under the radar.

Today I was reading cyclist Steve Roberts' advice on travel *(p. 249)*: Don't focus so much on your destination that you neglect to experience the richness of travel. The sights, the sounds, the weather, the landscape, the people....

"There ain't no journey what don't change you some."
        –David Mitchell

Got info on Rolling Homes to share?
We'll continue publishing on the subject, so contact us at ***shelter@shelterpub.com*** if you have or know of any unique rolling homes.

Photo by Kevin Slechta (see pp. 86–89)

Searching for Waves
Kerstin Bürk

"I began to chase adventures and dreams rather than money and status."

Even though Patscho is really small, there is enough space to welcome friends. Here three of my friends from primary school came to join me for part of my journey.

More . . .

HELLO LLOYD,
A friend sent me an article about your new *Rolling Homes* book project, and as you were asking for interesting homes on wheels, I thought you might be interested in my tiny home.

Growing up far from the ocean in southwest Germany, I started to surf late in life (age 20!). I discovered my love for the sea and a passion for riding waves.

Being dedicated to surfing changed my life completely. I was pulled into nature and the great unknown — where I began to chase adventures and dreams rather than money and status.

I began spending every free minute outside — traveling to find empty waves. While I was moving between many different places — from Australia to South America, as well as to Africa — I started to think about having a safe home-on-the-go.

It was this longing for a shelter, as well as for far-off surfing adventures, that led me to build a tiny home on wheels as my final thesis as an architectural student at The University of Stuttgart. I didn't have much money, but I had dreams of a home on wheels.

So I bought and converted a tiny Piaggio Porter, with little money to start. I developed a design that, with its multi-functions, allowed me to combine different spaces and needs.

You wouldn't think so, but besides basic needs, there was enough space for two sewing machines, my mobile jewelry workshop, and three surfboards. With this rolling home and workshop combined, I was ready to set off on a new adventure.

Everywhere I go people stop to have a closer look, take a photo, have a laugh, and tell me that's the smallest camper they have ever seen.

At first I didn't plan on traveling very far; however, I ended up rolling for 35,000 km (21,000 miles) for over two years along the Atlantic coast, between Ireland and Morocco.

On this journey I dedicated my time to surfing, creating, exploring, and connecting with people — as well as nature — but more importantly, connecting with myself. I soon realized it wasn't only the waves and a rooftop I was longing for.

I was escaping into the unknown to search for something deeper. Something that can be found very close without

traveling far. I found home, not only in my minivan Patscho but also within myself. A peaceful feeling of belonging, no matter where.

For a long time, *Happiness Is Homemade* was my little fashion brand's only slogan, but during my journey, it also became my motto in life and, finally, the title of a book in which I have written about travel experiences and thoughts, as well as DIY ideas and recipes for a happy journey through life. (*See Kerstin's website below.*)

My latest journey with Patscho made me stop rolling physically, but it turned out to be one of my best trips. When I was stuck in a two-month lockdown in Morocco, I met and fell in love with my boyfriend Jonathan and a Moroccan street dog named Jimmy. So I am no longer traveling alone.

That showed me once again that life is like surfing: if you go with the flow, you get the best rides.

koermi-koermet.com

Kerstin's book, *Happiness Is Homemade* (in English), contains DIY ideas, recipes and mindful thoughts for the road, as well as a little travelogue about her two-year journey, from *koermi-koermet.com*.

Slow-motion video of functions of the van: *koermi-koermet.com/minivan*

"It's a 2009 Piaggio Porter, total cost $3,225."

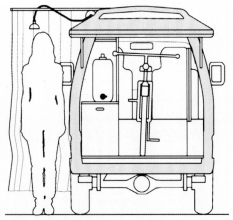

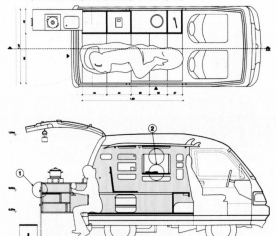

1. Höhenverstellbare Füße M 1:2

2 x 16mm 3-Schicht-Platte (Fichte)
beweglich verschraubt mit
M6 Flachrundschraube mit Vierkantsatz
durch
Langloch
verschraubt mit
M6 Flügelmutter

2. Klapptisch aus Regalwand

oben:
Schieberiegelverschluss

unten:
2 x 16mm 3-Schicht-Platte (Fichte)
beweglich verbunden durch
16mm Klavierband

"Being dedicated to surfing changed my life completely."

VITAL STATISTICS

- **Make and model:** 2009 Piaggio Porter
- **Tare weight:** 990 kg (2182 lbs.)
- **Displacement:** 1296 cm^3
- **Power:** 64 HP
- **Consumption:** 7L / 100km (33 mpg)
- **Max. speed:** 134 km/h (83 mph)
- **Fuel:** Super 95
- **Car cost:** 1,700 € ($2,025)
- **Outfitting costs:** approx. 1,000 € ($1,200)
- Outside shower tube
- No toilet
- No solar power

More...

One of the first rolling shop stands in the pine forest of France

"People tell me that it's the smallest camper they have ever seen."

"Life is like surfing: if you go with the flow, you get the best rides."

*Jonathan
and Kerstin
with Jimmy*

1988 Mitsubishi Delica: SlackerVan

Home, Office, and Transportation for YogaSlackers Sam and Raquel

Raquel Hernández-Cruz

W E'VE BEEN ASKED SEVERAL TIMES, "WHY TRAVEL?"
To us, this question is like asking someone, "Why breathe?"
Traveling is our way of life. I believe there are some people who can't grow roots in one place and thrive. This group—to whom we belong—must have inherited an ancestral nomadic gene.

Thousands of years ago, our ancestors survived thanks to their ability to be mobile and adaptable, and to travel on a daily basis. They experienced the world one day at a time, without set schedules and daily routines other than those set by biological needs.

That's us!

Sam has been living out of a vehicle since 2009. I joined him in 2012. We first lived out of a 1988 Ford Festiva. We roamed North America teaching yoga, slacklining, acroyoga, handstands, and led adventure-based retreats.

After five years living together in a tiny car, we decided to upgrade to a larger vehicle. Our requirements were simple: a larger bed and "negative" space to move around. Sam really wanted a 4×4 vehicle with a small footprint and had been keeping an eye on Mitsubishi Delicas. We were lucky to find one after a few days of searching.

ND • COLLECTOR
SLACKER
PEACE GARDEN STATE

Purchasing the Delica was the easy part. Making sure a 1988 vehicle worked perfectly was a different story.

When we bought the van, it had a faulty alternator. On our first trips, we had to stop and charge the battery once a day. But doing so meant we travelled slowly, slept inside our "new" seven-passenger van, and planned our build.

Shortly thereafter, the U-joint broke, taking with it the drive shaft and transfer case. Our previous experience living and fixing a 1988 Ford Festiva had given us the tools required, so we didn't freak out (at least not too much). "We got this," we thought. Five days later, we were ready to move again.

I wish I could say that building and maintaining a vehicle while living in it is easy. It's not. It's a challenge. But it works for us due to a vast array of friends across the U.S. willing to lend tools, garages, time, and skills.

Our first build took eleven days. We installed the first iteration of our roof rack system, electric system, kitchen layout, and bed frame in Rhode Island.

We knew we wanted to live in the van for a few months before finalizing the details, as what we had designed on paper had to be proven experientially—which was correct! After a few months, we decided to switch our under-the-bed storage system.

Our second build was in California. There we added a rag top (to access the roof boxes from the inside of the van), and redid the bed frame and storage areas.

"We've been asked, 'Why travel?' To us, this is like asking someone, 'Why breathe?'"

We spent a lot of time adding a pop-out extension to the driver's side of the van. This allowed us to add an Arctic Tern double-pane window to easily vent the van while cooking and, most importantly, to switch our sleeping position from long ways in the van to sideways.

At that time, it was almost a year since we had bought the van and we hadn't yet taken any major trips.

After installing an air compressor, we hit the road and traveled all the way to the Arctic Circle. This tour allowed us to test our systems and decide what else needed improvement. A little over a year later we returned to California, where we spent six months—during the pandemic—making a new set of improvements.

I wish I could say the build is done. But we now realize that as long as we continue traveling in this van, we will continue "seeing" new ways to make it more comfortable, functional, and mechanically sound. That's part of the fun!

We remind ourselves to bookend each build with a major trip. That allows us to feed both our need to travel and our need to have the "perfect" home in the making. Our plan is to continue traveling and building the most modified Mitsubishi Delica out there.

Vital Statistics
Sam and Raquel have a huge list of modifications listed at:
www.yogaslackers.com/nomadlife/slackervan

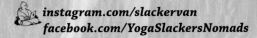
instagram.com/slackervan
facebook.com/YogaSlackersNomads

"Traveling is our way of life."

More...

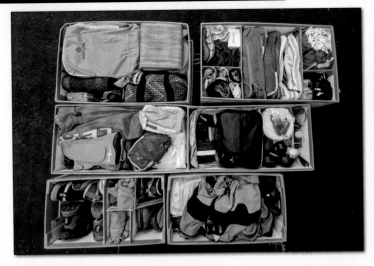

"After installing an air compressor, we hit the road and traveled all the way to the Arctic Circle."

"Our plan is to continue traveling and building the most modified Mitsubishi Delica out there."

A Van Called Perry

Ashley Harris

Photos by April Harris

OFTEN PEOPLE DO NOT FOLLOW their dreams because they are trapped in a bubble. Whether it's a mundane 9-to-5 job, relationships, or insecurities — we have to know that there is always a way out.

My way out came in the form of a 1984 Chevy Travelcraft van named Perry. I'm a huge vintage lover so when I was searching for a RV I knew I wanted something older. Perry is everything I dreamed of and more!

He is all original and was kept in immaculate condition before I got him. I love everything about Perry, from the antique mercury glass closet doors to the '80s brown color that is so often despised. In my heart, I feel like this RV was made exactly for me!

Perry not only gives me the freedom to travel the world but also allows me to fully focus on bettering myself as a person and as a fashion designer.

If I were working every day just to pay bills, how much time would I have to create? If I were working every day just to keep a roof over my head, when would I actually have time to enjoy my home? Is my home even "my" home if I'm renting? Those are all questions and feelings that I battled with in the past.

Now my days are much simpler and more fulfilling. Less is definitely more! Sustainability comes easily! Inspiration from nature, wildlife, and different cultures flow through me daily. I use my inspirations to create art and I sell my art along the way to make money.

One day when Perry is ready to retire from life on the road, I will purchase land and we will settle down there. On the land I'll build my own tiny home, eat only the food that I grow, and raise all types of farm animals. Ahhh, I can see it now!

When I used to hear the word "abundance," I would automatically think of money and wealth. I've learned that abundance is not something that we acquire. Abundance is simply a manifestation of one's desires. My life is truly abundant.

"He is all original and was kept in immaculate condition before I got him."

VITAL STATISTICS

- **Vehicle:** 1989 Chevy Travelcraft
- **Engine:** 5.7L V8 350
- **Chassis:** Chevy van G30
- **Mileage:** 58,657
- **Full bathroom:** Shower, tub, sink, toilet
- **Kitchen:** 4-burner stove, Magic Chef oven, fridge, freezer, furnace, dinette with storage under each bench
- 2 vents/fans, cruise control, backup cam, awning
- 3 sleeping areas, tons and tons of storage all over, generator, stereo system

"Sustainability comes easily!"

Advice: Sometimes when people get an older RV, they automatically rip out the insides, even if there's nothing wrong. I'd advise you not to get caught up in what other people are doing or what other people's rigs look like. Be you and the rest will fall into place.

instagram.com/rolling_sess
www.AmarieCollections.com
www.youtube.com/channel/UCCr_Au-pYnBtisHetGdhziw

"I truly feel like this RV was made exactly for me!"

More...

"Inspiration from nature, wildlife, and different cultures flow through me daily."

"Perry…allows me to fully focus on bettering myself as a person and as a fashion designer."

"My life is truly abundant."

15

Toyota Sienna Van

Travis Skinner

This is a simple, practical consideration for anyone contemplating a van. Web research indicates that Sienna vans often go for 200,000–300,000 miles, and get combined city/highway mileage of over 20 miles per gallon. I've been considering getting a used one (for one thing, in case we have to evacuate due to fire danger), and reportedly 2010, 2015, and 2017 models get high ratings for durability.

Travis' home, called The Leafspring, in which everything, including steel and copper parts, is handcrafted, was featured in Small Homes *(pp. 52–53). On his website (**www.100handed.org**) other examples of his work can be seen, including an amazing sculptural sauna covered with copper shingles, and most recently, a unique book on the project titled* Anglerfish Sauna: Material Based Design & Deep Sea Sculpture.   –LK

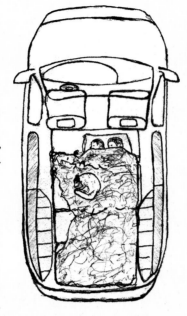

O H LITTLE TOYOTA VAN,
    your fill is never through.
So many mountains of materials,
    so many country roads that you flew.
This vessel holds humble wonder,
    without drawing attention to her door.
A modern-day magic carpet,
    with a three-inch foam mattress floor.
There is a simple freedom;
    mobility allows us to view
When the setting sun rests in the sea,
    and when we pour the morning brew.
This cocoon is our container,
    an extension of our handmade nest,
A grocery getter, camouflaged chameleon,
    bringing hope to our next quest.

Build by Travis Skinner
instagram.com/pairoducks
www.100handed.org

Photos by Macky Swoboda
instagram.com/mackyswob

"A modern day magic carpet…"

"There is a simple freedom; / mobility allows us to view /
When the setting sun rests in the sea."

A Van Named Spock
Kirk Williams

"My van, Spock, evolved through a 10-year R&D using other vehicles."

I was stunned when I saw Kirk's photos on Instagram. I contacted him and was delighted to hear back.

After receiving his photos (over 100 of them) and story, I had a problem. How was I going to make a selection so as not to end up with 32 pages on his life and adventures? There really could be a book on just Kirk and his trusty Spock.

So I've edited things down to tell the story of this unique guy and his wonderful sense of optimism, spirit of adventure, and joy in life, which certainly come shining through here, despite the challenges.

As the other Kirk said of the voyages of the starship Enterprise: "To boldly go where no man has gone before!"

—LK

MY LIFE IS FULL OF OBSTACLES. Whether it's tall grass, steep curbs, thick carpets, or spring-loaded bathroom doors, nearly everything is challenging to a quadriplegic.

"Not being able to use your legs is one thing," I've often said. "But not having any dexterity in your hands or fingers is a whole other level!"

Even wheelchair-accessible hotel rooms are far from easy! Light switches I can't turn off, towels out of reach, blinds I can't shut, etc. So what's the solution?

Creating a home on wheels that I designed to make my life as easy as possible! With it I can travel and see the world, while having all my necessities on my back.

My van, Spock, evolved through a 10-year R&D using other vehicles. From what chassis would be ideal for international travel to what light switches would be easiest for me to use, no detail was too small.

Spock's foundation is built on a 2017 Ford Transit medium-roof 148-inch wheelbase van with a Quigley 4×4 conversion. I chose this platform because the transit is offered with a 3.5 liter twin turbo gas motor known as the Ecoboost.

While a diesel motor would be more ideal in a lot of ways, the U.S. models are unable to run on low-sulfur diesel — making them essentially useless for global travel. The medium roof height gives me more than enough head space inside and is just barely short enough to squeeze into a high-roof shipping container for secure international transport. These two details were critical in designing something I could use anywhere in the world.

The Quigley 4×4 conversion was something I knew could be utilized for the types of travel I prefer. I love getting off the beaten path and finding remote campsites. I also know that getting my van stuck would be more than a minor inconvenience for me. I can't just walk down the trail to go find help or dig myself out of the sand. Chances are, if the van is stuck — I would be too.

That said, I still equipped Spock with a Warn winch on the front and carry the necessary recovery gear with me whenever I'm pushing my limits. Usually, if I'm going to do anything risky, I bring companions along to help should we get stuck.

One of the modifications that I get the most questions about is the lift that hoists me inside the vehicle. This lift is known as the SuperArm lift. I chose this particular unit because of its simplicity and the fact that it doesn't block the entire doorway like a traditional platform lift.

What's unique about the SuperArm is that it clips to my wheelchair and swings me in and out of the van rather than my riding a platform or ramp up. Since it doesn't have a platform, it will literally set me down on any type of terrain — it doesn't care. I also require much less space to get in and out of the vehicle than with a platform lift.

Once inside Spock, the design focuses on functionality. A sink that my knees can roll under, for instance, makes it much easier for me to do dishes and also allows space for me to turn around without running into anything.

Drawers bring items within reach without my having core strength. My refrigerator is mounted up high where I can use two hands to grab heavy items such as milk or juice without dexterity. A bed in the back is at the exact height that I know I can transfer to from my chair. Everything has a purpose.

The fold-down induction cooktop was incorporated because my mobility driver's seat requires so much space for me to transfer to from my wheelchair. The cooktop can be folded down during transport but positioned upright for cooking once I'm at camp. The driver's seat also has a 180-degree swivel, allowing another seat for someone to use the stove or to relax and look out the door.

Without the use of my legs, I drive Spock using a right-angle hand-control system. Basically, there's a lever to the left of my steering wheel that if I pushed towards the floor, activates the throttle; and if I pushed towards the dashboard, applies the brake. Additionally, I have a tri-pin steering knob on the steering wheel that holds my right wrist to control the wheel without grip. This may sound complicated but you actually get used to it pretty quick.

What I have found is that by having a place to sleep, eat, go to the bathroom in, and drive, I'm mostly as capable as any other person out there. Because of this, I've traveled up to Alaska, all around the United States, into Mexico, and around Patagonia in Argentina and Chile. My life is easy within the van; it's once I get outside that things get complicated! Spock, my freedom pod, has given me back a sense of adventure and independence that I could not have had any other way.

When I first broke my neck, my biggest fear was that I wasn't going to be able to get out into nature and see the world anymore. Now I've realized it can still be done; I just need the right tools to do it. Thanks to my home on wheels, I am able to experience more than I'd have ever thought possible.

For more information or with any questions about adapting a vehicle, check out **@impact.overland** on Instagram or **www.ImpactOverland.com**.

See you down the road.

—Kirk

instagram.com/impact.overland
www.ImpactOverland.com

More...

"I love getting off the beaten path and finding remote campsites."

"I can't just walk down the trail to go find help or dig myself out of the sand."

More...

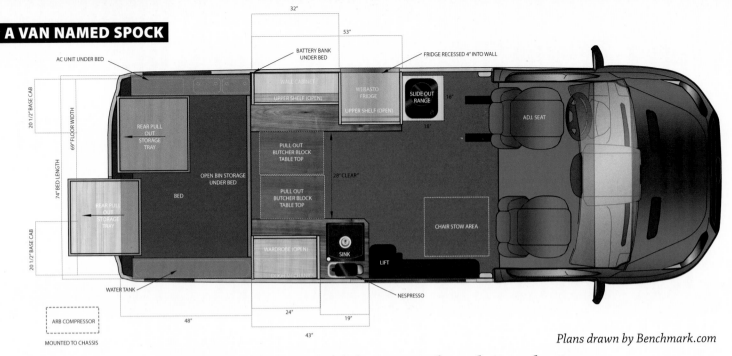

32"

53"

BATTERY BANK UNDER BED

FRIDGE RECESSED 4" INTO WALL

AC UNIT UNDER BED

20 1/2" BASE CAB

69" FLOOR WIDTH

WALL CABINET

UPPER SHELF (OPEN)

WEBASTO FRIDGE

SLIDE OUT RANGE

16"

ADJ. SEAT

18"

REAR PULL OUT STORAGE TRAY

74" BED LENGTH

UPPER SHELF (OPEN)

OPEN BIN STORAGE UNDER BED

PULL OUT BUTCHER BLOCK TABLE TOP

28" CLEAR

BED

REAR PULL OUT STORAGE TRAY

PULL OUT BUTCHER BLOCK TABLE TOP

CHAIR STOW AREA

20 1/2" BASE CAB

WARDROBE (OPEN)

SINK

LIFT

WATER TANK

NESPRESSO

ARB COMPRESSOR

48"

24"

19"

MOUNTED TO CHASSIS

43"

Plans drawn by Benchmark.com

"*Not being able to use your legs is one thing, but not having any dexterity in your hands or fingers is a whole other level!*"

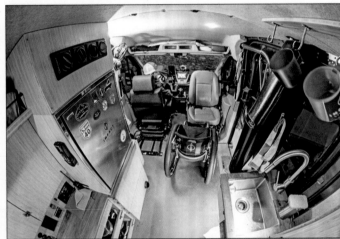

"*Drawers bring items within reach without my having core strength.*"

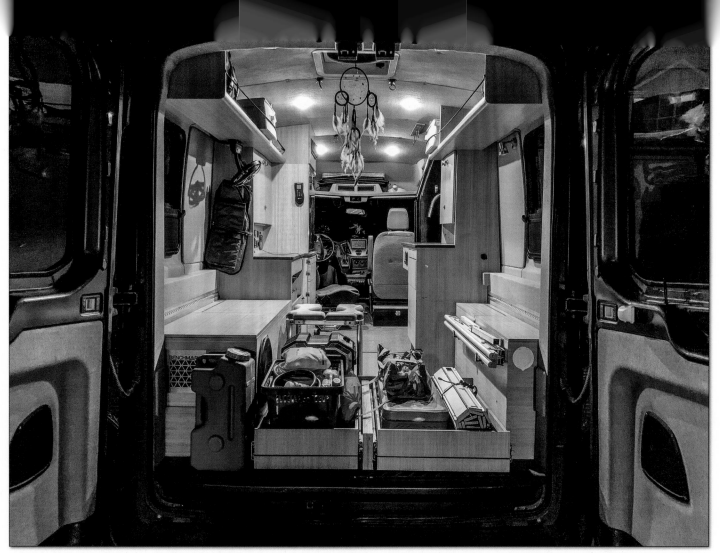

"Once inside Spock, the design focuses on functionality."

"My life is easy within the van; it's once I get outside that things get complicated!"   **More...**

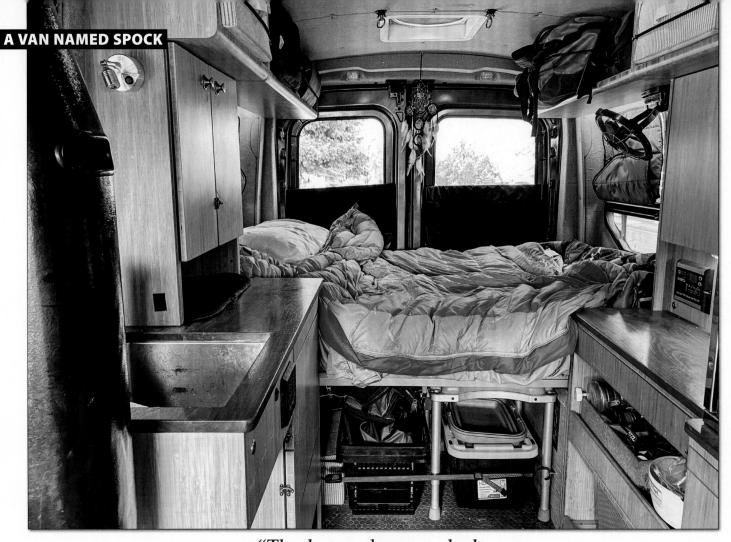

*"Thanks to my home on wheels,
I am able to experience more
than I'd have ever thought possible."*

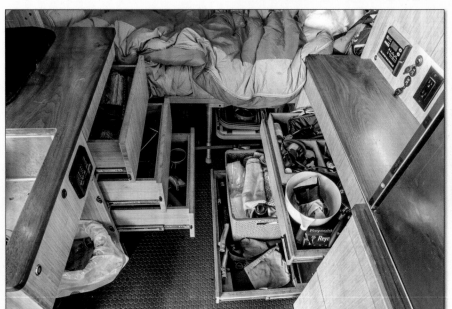

Wheelchair wheel locks in place.

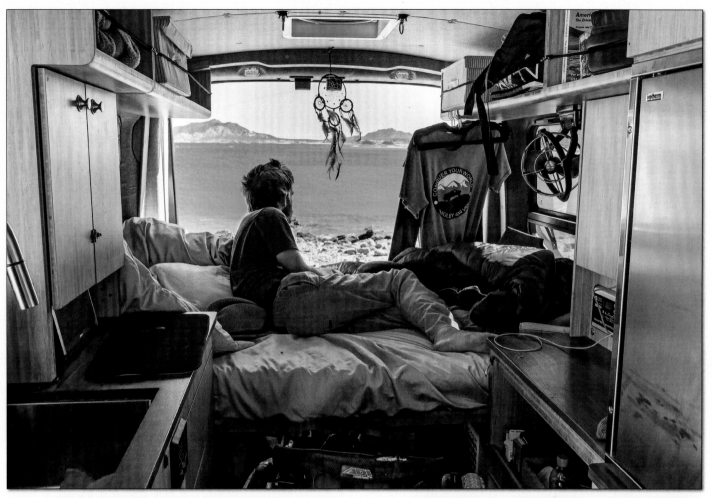

"I've traveled up to Alaska, all around the United States, into Mexico, and around Patagonia in Argentina and Chile."

Mountains, Valleys, Islands, and the Sea
Ana de la Montaña & Christoph Wallner

> *"Ana asked, 'Are you really sure we can build something like this?'"*

(Ana is Spanish; Christoph is Austrian.)

ALL THE GOOD STORIES THAT WE were listening to, watching, and reading started off with a van. So we bought one. That's literally how it started.

Having not really worked much with our hands before (we only trained our fingertips in office jobs), we started working on our van not only to get on the road but to learn some new skills as well.

I remember sitting in a restaurant with Ana right after we bought our Opel Movano (owned by a roofer before). We were watching a conversion video on YouTube, and Ana asked, "Are you really sure we can build something like this?"

From that day on, we were motivated, and we spent all our spare time building this mobile home that we now call Movi. Knowing that we should prepare for all seasons, we insulated and soundproofed the interior. (Austria, our homeland, can be pretty cold in winter.) We installed a

heater, built the furniture, got a big solar panel, and installed a water system.

Then, in November 2019, we took off and escaped from the rhythm of everyday life. We climbed with friends in Sardinia, ski-toured the Pyrenees mountains, surfed the Atlantic coasts of France, Spain, and Portugal, climbed and skied on the highest mountains of Morocco, and explored all seven Canary Islands.

One of our main goals was to be more active in our favorite sports (skiing, surfing, running, and climbing), but we realized that we also needed to relearn how to calm down and not follow schedules In addition, we needed to take days off from traveling to reflect on our adventures.

Now, when we think about our two years on the road, we remember the countless campfires in the Moroccan desert and sharing endless waves with the crazy surf rats we met in northern Spain.

We shiver recalling the snow-covered mountains of Andorra where we ski-toured out of our camper and returned to a warm and cozy home after long days in the snow.

We won't forget those crazy landscapes on the Canary Islands and the animals we rescued, adopted, and sheltered. (Yes, that happens regularly if your companion is a veterinarian — in Sardinia, we even needed to rescue a goat that had fallen into a steep well, believe it or not!)

Not even the COVID-19 pandemic, which of course changed all our plans, stopped us. In the middle of a medieval and incredible landscape outside Cáceres (Spain), we found shelter in a country home where we slowed down for four months.

We don't really know where we will be when this book gets released, but if we could have one wish, it would be "on the road." And if nothing crazy happens before then, that's where we'll be.

In the mountains of Picos de Europa

"Then, in November 2019, we took off
and escaped from the rhythm of everyday life."

More...

VITAL STATISTICS

- **Vehicle:** 2013 Opel Movano 2.3 dti, L2 H2, diesel van, bought with 100,000km (62,000 mi.) on it; now 150,000km — 93,200 mi.).

- **Outside:** Homemade roof rack, 300W solar panel, 180 × 45 × 35 cm (72˝ × 18˝ × 13´) sheet metal box with lockers for three surfboards

- **Inside:** Insulated with 20mm Armaflex tube insulation, soundproofed with Alubutyl. All furniture is made out of 12mm (½˝) beech plywood. Ceiling is made out of special pine wood from Austria. Cross bed is 182cm × 140cm (72˝ long by 55˝ wide). The "garage" is a storage box, with the water tank, two batteries, and lots of space for our sports equipment. The kitchen has a mobile double-burner gas stove, a sink with hot and cold water, a slidable refrigerator (compressor), and lots of space for food and dishes. The passenger seat is turnable and there is a safe for our valuables. There is one skylight and one side window.

- **Water:** We use a 90L (24 gal.) water tank that fits around the wheelhouse. A 6L (6.3 qt.) water boiler (Elgena Nautic Compact) runs with electricity or through our diesel heater. The water tank provides water for our outdoor shower and the sink.

- **Electricity:** 300W solar panel, 2 100Ah AGM batteries; a charging booster is connected to the van's alternator so it charges while driving. A self-made controlling board with marine on and off switches.

- **Toilet:** Porta Potti and we add chemical-free and biodegradable odor neutralizer.

- **Heating:** Diesel heater, Planar 44D-12 4kW air heater, that uses fuel from the tank

What info can we pass along to people building or outfitting a vehicle?

Focus on usability. Try to design everything that is simple, so it needs only one move to reach, open, or store. Most important things for us (and all our van-dweller friends) are toilet, water, electricity, and gas. Everything else is secondary. Check the internet for ideas and try to fit components to your needs.

What would you do differently if you had it to do over again?

A permanent stove in the kitchen. The mobile stove was meant to be used for cooking inside and outside. The longer we travelled, the less we cooked outside. Wind, weather, and police are against it.

 www.instagram.com/movi_hygge

"We won't forget those crazy landscapes on the Canary Islands and the animals we rescued, adopted, and sheltered."

Surfing in Portugal

"We remember the countless campfires in the Moroccan desert and sharing endless waves with the crazy surf rats we met in northern Spain."

Ski Touring in Morocco

Converted Ford Transit Van
Jesús Sierra

"All in all, it was four months on the road and about 6,500 land miles, plus another 2,500 on the sea."

Bardenas Reales, Spain

More...

In 2015, I got an email from Jesús, saying:

"I became a carpenter / timber framer / ecobuilder in my early 30s because of your books. About 15 years ago I was working in an office and I got *Shelter* and I was hooked. Then *Home Work* came out and got me going. Made me realize that I didn't want to live in a conventional house anymore. When *Builders of the Pacific Coast* came out, I knew that building was my future.

Now I build shelter for people who want something different but can't afford to pay a contractor. I fit out narrow boats, caravans, camper vans, build wooden yurts in the woods, and small trailers on farms. The poor have the right to live in nice homes too..."

Two of Jesús' creations were featured in our book Small Homes: *a beautiful yurt framed with rough larch rafters in the English woods and a small woodland home in southwest England (pp. 62–65).*

Jesús and I have kept in touch. He journeyed from England to Scotland to attend a presentation I did in Edinburgh in 2015, and he has become friends with Yogan, a French carpenter whose creations have appeared in our last three building books (and in this one on pp. 168–173, 180–181, and 214–217).

Recently Jesús and Anna bought land and an old stone house on the island of La Palma in the Canary Islands (off the north coast of Africa). They are rebuilding the house and have planted 50 fruit trees. —LK

MY VAN ROSE AND I HAVE BEEN together since 2006. She's a 1996 Ford Transit, 2.5 liter diesel engine, with 80 horsepower.

I did the conversion in a couple of months and lived in her full-time until 2010. I travelled extensively through Europe during the winters and lived and worked as a carpenter in Bristol the rest of the year.

My daughter, Juniper, was born in May, 2018, and my partner, Anna, and I decided to take advantage of her one-year maternity leave and go traveling for a few months.

As one of my customers wanted a tree house built on the island of La Palma in the Canary islands, we left Britain in November, 2018. We crossed France and mainland Spain and got on a ferry for 63 long hours at sea.

Black Forest, Germany

"She's a 1996 Ford Transit, 2.5 liter diesel engine, with 80 hp."

We spent six weeks in La Palma and built the outer shell of the tree house. Afterwards we crossed to the even smaller island of El Hierro. After three weeks there we crossed back to mainland Spain and carried on through Portugal, France (staying for a few days at Yogan's place), Germany (visiting some friends), Luxembourg, Belgium, and finally a short ferry crossing back to the United Kingdom.

All in all, it was four months on the road and about 6,500 land miles, plus another 2,500 on the sea.

In her present state, Rose has a 70-liter (18½ gallon) water tank, a Whale Gusher Mk3 bilge pump, a mini compost toilet, and a sofa that slides out into a full double bed, which is 1.35 meters wide by 1.9 meters long (4½ × 6.2 feet) and meets a shoe chest that doubles up as a cot for Juniper.

All lighting is warm white SMDs, powered from a 135 Ah AGM battery and a 150-watt monocrystalline solar panel. The regulator is an old-fashioned but totally reliable Steca PR2020.

Insulation is sheep's wool, and cladding is mostly spruce, with some London plane, ash, and oak as details.

Last but not least is a small but feisty Parp Industrie wood burner that keeps us toasty even in the coldest nights of winter.

Although she's not a 4×4, the wheels are really big so the clearance is over 60cm (24 inches). Despite driving on dirt tracks very often (some quite rough), I've never hit the ground in all these years. This has allowed us to frequently drive to pretty remote spots, well away from the reach of motor homes.

Traveling with a baby puts a totally new perspective on van life. The sleepless nights and the demands of a really lively little girl are hugely outweighed by the pleasures of seeing her growing and changing every day and of spending most of our time together out in nature. Although we might move often and meet lots of new people almost every day, she always knows where her home is at the end of the day. A really happy, nomadic baby!

*"All lighting is warm white SMDs,
powered from a 135 Ah AGM battery
and a 150-watt monocrystalline solar panel."*

*"A really happy,
nomadic baby!"*

Cold winter evening, Alto Tajo, Spain

We Built a Life

Emmett & Katy Nelson

I BUILT MYRTLE AFTER SAWING OFF the back top half of a Ford work van while living in the garage of a climbing gym in Seattle, Washington. I learned to weld and rivet, and salvage aluminum metal sheeting and supplies from all over the west coast.

My fiancee Katy and I have lived in this van for around three years and have really enjoyed learning to work and adjust to this one-of-a-kind living space.

I was inspired by Lloyd Kahn, Jay Nelson, Foster Huntington, and countless friends helping along the way.

It's a 2002 Ford Econoline V8 Triton with 154,000 miles. It has an RV full oven with three-burner stove, a large Zhune sink with running water, three-inch-thick live edge counters, and a lighting system.

We have a foot-pump shower in the back barn-door storage area, which holds all of our climbing, fishing, and surfing gear, skateboards, and such. We have a canopy that is currently detached.

We've had such fun learning and making mistakes — as is bound to happen, but the outcome has helped us to discover how rewarding it is to create something together.

We'd be thrilled to try another build, although we have a few different versions we'd like to see come to fruition, as we are expecting to grow our little family.

instagram.com/ibuiltavan
instagram.com/webuiltalife
instagram.com/emmettnelson1
instagram.com/honeymaes
instagram.com/honeyflowstudios

"I learned to weld and rivet, and salvage aluminum metal sheeting."

*"The outcome has helped us understand
how rewarding it is to create something together."*

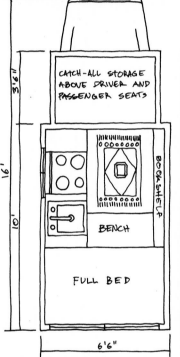

CATCH-ALL STORAGE
ABOVE DRIVER AND
PASSENGER SEATS

3'6"

6'

10'

BOOKSHELF

BENCH

FULL BED

6'6"

Crystal's AdVANturous Life

Crystal Vanner

"I am a 50-year-old Black, solo woman nomad presently in a 1995 Ford E150 conversion van with 108,000 miles.

Looking to live a more adVANtureous life, live more minimally, live more free, and live more on less [income]."

I SET OFF ON AUGUST 27, 2015. I DECIDED to start my journey in my native northern Virginia area while still working my public school system job. I started out in the SUV I already owned, a 2000 GMC Jimmy (SUV). I worked to afford mechanical repairs on it and save for a van.

I finally found a decent, affordable minivan at the end of 2015, and again I was working to mechanically repair a vehicle while living in it.

In 2017, I decided I'd lived a "stationary nomad life" long enough, and in September, I set out for Maine. I traveled slowly, stopping along the way to see sites, to meet my YouTube subscribers, and to pick up odd jobs on Craigslist to fund my travels. That October, I was westward bound for the first time and haven't looked back!

I've crossed the country four times, have only 12 of the lower 48 states left to travel to…mostly colder weather states, and am currently in my fourth vehicle/van home (during the 2020 Covid-19 pandemic).

It hasn't always been easy or safe being solo, a woman, and Black. I've learned a lot about myself. I have gained knowledge, experience, and strength that comes with traveling this country alone.

I've managed to build friendships and nomad connections on both coasts. I have had ups and downs, but I wouldn't give it up for anything. My YouTube subscribers are the most genuine and supportive people you could find.

"I've crossed the country four times now, have only 12 of the lower 48 states left to travel to…"

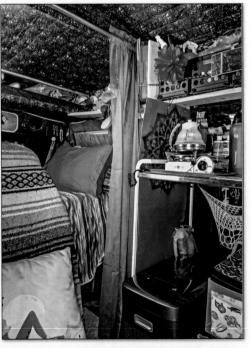

"I've managed to build friendships and nomad connections on both coasts."

I want *everyone*, especially other people of color, to know that this lifestyle doesn't have to be a future dream — it can happen now. This life doesn't have to look like a perfect social media picture. I've been parked right next to expensive Sprinters, $100k+ RVs, and professionally built-out vans/skoolies*/rigs … but *we all had the same view.*

Enjoy the journey of life.

CrystalVanner.com
youtube.com/CrystalVanner
instagram.com/crystalvanner

———

__skoolies:__ slang for people living in buses

"*This lifestyle doesn't have to be a future dream — it can happen now.*"

Two Sprinter Vans
Greg Watson and Valerie Velardi

Mercedes Sprinter vans converted to RVs are popular these days among the nomadascenti. Top-of-the-line, off-the-shelf, is the Winnebago Revel 4×4, which is priced at $175–$200,000 in 2022. Not so much compared to buying a new home in California, but still…

I chose these two Sprinters, outfitted by Greg Watson, for their simplicity and practicality.

Valerie's van as an example of a home-crafted rig for its thoughtful design as a vehicle "not intended for full-time residence," and Greg's excellent craftsmanship.

Greg's own van is an example of a traveling carpenter's rig, with Mercedes quality.

Very important with both vans: you can stand up inside.

Note: *See Foster Huntington's experience and subsequent thoughts on Sprinter vans* *on page 48.*

Greg wrote the following.   –LK

Vehicle: 2015 Mercedes Sprinter Passenger, with windows all the way around. This gives it the light and airy feeling Valerie wanted. The factory tint is dark enough for privacy during the day, and there's a full set of insulated window covers for nighttime.

Engine: 3.0L V6 diesel; averaging about 22 mpg all around. We kept the van pretty light in added materials, and she's careful not to carry more than she needs. This also makes it easy to stay organized.

Batteries: Two Lifeline 220Ah AGM batteries as power for the house systems. In spring of 2018, lithium would have been triple in price. As the price of lithium comes down, we'll probably convert for the greater useable capacity.

Charging: The batteries are charged through a Kisae Abso DMT1250 DC–DC charger, which takes input from both the van's alternator and sends a 50 amp max to the batteries, and also has an MPPT charger for the 300W of solar panels on the roof.

Solar: Three 100W Renogy panels designed for 12V charging. The panels are attached with CNC aluminum mounts specifically designed by ***DIYVan.com***. (They have many great products.)

Inverter: Kisae 2000W pure sine inverter powers three AC outlets, all with built-in USB outlets. The larger inverter can power a hair dryer and electric kettle.

Ventilation: Two Maxxair 7200 fans on the ceiling, one that pushes air in and the other pulling the air out to create a breeze: useful in hot climates like the desert in summer.

For colder climates, a diesel heater produces quiet, dry heat. It sips fuel from the van's fuel tank (about 0.2 liters per hour), and the fan draws only a couple of amps — and Valerie can come back to a warm, dry van after swimming in the bay.

The walls are insulated with 3m Thinsulate; a version designed for vehicles that not only insulates, but also absorbs road noise.

Galley: Dometic sink/stove combo with glass lid. The faucet (cold-water only) folds down when not in use

Cooking: Two small propane burners hooked to a standard 5 lb. bottle clipped under the sink

Water: 6-gallon jerry can under sink, which drains into another jerry can. They are removable and can be filled (and emptied) anywhere, unlike built-in tanks.

Fridge: Standard small dorm fridge that runs off inverter. Not as efficient as a 12V fridge, but it was a fifth of the cost, and the power use hasn't been an issue.

Lighting: Valerie prefers warm dimmable lighting, so I chose warm white LEDs. The main lighting is a dimmable strip under the overhead cabinet; there's also an LED strip recessed into the ceiling overhead panel that gives a brighter light when needed. For getting up in the night-time, I inset strips of amber LEDs into the cabinet toe kick strips.

Sleeping: I'm proud of the bed design. It's like the couch/bed in most VW campers, a back seat that folds flat to become the bed. Valerie wanted the bed to sit longways in the van, but to avoid the mattress taking up so much space during the day, so I designed a platform that uses a mattress that folds up at the forward one-third.

During the day there's a bench seat in front of the folded mattress, and the height of the folded mattress provides a decent back rest. (*In the photo of Greg and Valerie above, the bench is on their left.*) For sleeping, electric motors raise up the bed and a platform slides out from underneath.

When the bed is lowered back down, the mattress folds forward, and a full-size mattress is ready for use. The mattress can be folded while the sheets are made up, so the whole affair takes but a few minutes. Below the bed is a safe that is bolted to the floor and is large enough for a laptop.

Porta Potti: Removable plastic Thetford Porta Potti in a cabinetry box; when the top is closed, it's a seat. The Thetford (which has a handle) can be taken outside if privacy is desired.

Cabinets are made from a combination of aluminum T-slot channel (from ***8020.net***) and bamboo plywood. 8020 is easy to cut with standard saws, and isn't hard to take apart if you change your mind.

Valerie's Van

The Design works very well for her use, which is I think pretty common for people who want a van that's not a full-time residence. Valerie gets compliments every time she opens the doors. The layout is simple and uncomplicated. There's no attempt to cram in a shower or a full-flush potty.

Valerie spends most of her time living in it while visiting her grandkids or friends, and a shower or flush toilet is often easily within reach. For her, it's a little private room when she visits her family and she can have her own space and live at her own pace.

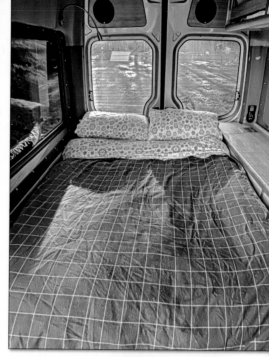

For sleeping, electric motors raise up the bed and a platform is slid out from underneath (looking in towards rear).

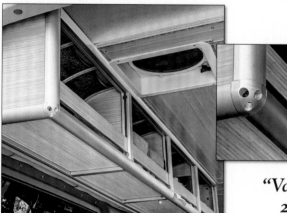

"Valerie averages about 22 mpg all around."

"There's no attempt to cram in a shower or a full-flush potty."

Greg's Van

In the '80s, Lew Lewandowski had a 1971 VW Westphalia van, in which he carried all his carpentry tools, including a mini table saw, as well as mechanic's tools and jacks so that he could drop the engine and rebuild it anywhere. He also slept and cooked in it (and had his two dogs) — a combination home/shop on wheels.

I always thought this was an option for a young builder. Take carpentry jobs as you travel around — self-contained. —LK

The Traveling Carpenter

Katie's Van Life
Katie Larsen

I'M A 27-YEAR-OLD NOMAD WHO HAS SERIOUS addictions to hot sauce, puzzling, and salt and vinegar chips. I've been living full-time on the road in various vans since 2017, documenting my travels online as *So We Bought A Van*.

I decided I wanted to pursue travel full-time and experience real freedom in my life. I began in a Mercedes Sprinter and now reside in a Ford Transit. Both van builds were DIY, with the Sprinter taking six months to complete and the Transit taking nine months.

Over the last five years, I traveled all over North America, including driving all the way to Alaska, all around Canada, all 49 lower states, and even spent some time in Baja California, Mexico.

My passion for the outdoors has grown immensely over the years, making stationary life feel just about impossible.

Some of my travels have included a partner, but most of my experiences on the road have been solo. These days, I have a five-year-old rescue dog named Indi as my co-pilot.

I began freelancing in 2017 and have loved working remotely since then. My days are balanced between work and play, mixed with a fair amount of self-care.

Many days are spent exploring trails in the mountains, visiting national and state parks, or finding epic swimming holes. If there's a body of water nearby, I'm probably swimming in it.

Life on the road means having the freedom to do what feels best to me, without any obligations or limitations. Being mobile allows me to pursue happiness and experience the world in such a deep capacity, spending almost every day in nature. It's amazing what living outside can do for the soul.

instagram.com/soweboughtavan
facebook.com/soweboughtavan
www.soweboughtavan.com
www.soweboughtavan.com/van-life-shop
youtube.com/channel/UCQBM_Lq4XVpGzd2x8YGPT-Q

> *"I decided I wanted to pursue travel full-time and experience real freedom in my life."*

VITAL STATISTICS

- **Vehicle:** 2016 Ford Transit, 148" wheelbase, 38,000 mi. This is my second DIY build, but the third van I've lived in. (Most of the photos here are of my previous vehicle, a Sprinter van.) I've always preferred a high-roof van and a stationary bed. Having a decent-size fridge helps in staying off-grid longer. So does having a good electrical system. My new van has a dining room table/workstation, which has been a gamechanger since I freelance remotely full-time. It also has a heater — a luxury but makes living in a van full-time easier during winter. So does having a composting toilet!

- **Ceiling fan:** Maxxair/Airxcel Deluxe 7500 K (smoke)

- **Stove/oven:** Dometic CU-434 propane 3-burner stainless steel stove/oven

- **Fridge:** Dometic CRX 110S

- **Solar kit:** Renogy 300W, 12V off-grid Premium Eclipse solar panel and DCC50S 12V 50A DC-DC onboard battery charger with MPPT

- **Batteries:** Two VMAXTANKS LFPGC2-12175 LiFePO4 Lithium-iron 12V 175Ah deep-cycle batteries

- **Inverter:** Renogy 2000W 12V pure sine wave inverter

- **Insulation:** Mix of spray foam, Thinsulate, and XPS foam board

- **Heater:** Espar/Eberspacher Airtronic B4L (petrol)

- **Table:** Lagun table-mount system

- **Toilet:** Air Head composting toilet & straight fan shroud

- **Tires:** BF Goodrich K02 all-terrain tires

- **Outdoor shower:** Portable handheld camping shower with 5 gal. water — 12V cigarette adapter

- **Water system:** Four Reliance Products Aqua-Tainer (7 gal. each)

"I freelance remotely full-time."

"It's amazing what living outside can do for the soul."

"My passion for the outdoors has grown immensely over the years, making stationary life feel just about impossible."

Custom Jeep Camper
Paul Jensen

When we started gathering info for this book a few years ago, we got an email from Paul Jensen, who had done a beautiful job outfitting a Sprinter van that was featured in Tiny Homes on the Move (pp. 10–11). Paul said he had modified a 2007 Jeep Wrangler Rubicon that had originally been outfitted as an Earthroamer expedition vehicle.

I did a little research and found out that most Earthroamers bought new these days are in the mid-$600,000 range. Not only that, but their HP truck is $1.7 million—yikes!

On the other hand, here is the story of a 63-year-old surfer creating his own version of an Earthroamer.

When I asked Paul recently for his curriculum vitae, he replied:

"Surfer, surfboard builder, teacher of building wood surfboards, general contractor, remodeler, cabinet maker, stair builder, vehicle customizer, consultant/designer for Homegrown Trailers; husband/father …provocateur…"

Paul also builds beautiful, wooden, hollow surfboards that are not only functional, but works of art.

—LK

"XV-JP #03 gets
a lot of attention."

More…

JEEPS HAVE BEEN AROUND FOREVER— Jeep campers not so. The company, Earthroamer builds expedition vehicles. Rumor was that Jeep would come out with a diesel motor, and for Earthroamer, that would make it suitable for an expedition vehicle. Accordingly, they made thirteen "XV-JPs" (with standard V6 gas motors). Then the rumor of diesel was squashed, and Earthroamer moved their focus to BIG campers.

XV-JP #03 was purchased second-hand by Mike Hiscox, who hired good people to improve it. I was one of those people. From the stock Earthroamer, we changed it radically. It's a long story: too long for here.

Mike had it for over a year when he sent it off for a major rear cabin modification that went horribly wrong. It's another long story, but eventually, he had to trailer it back home where it sat, in pieces, without a roof. Mike could have sold it as is for parts, or have had it rebuilt. Instead, he gifted it to me and I took a year setting it up as you see it.

Imagine almost any outdoor activity and this vehicle can get you there; and with the 40-gallon fuel capacity, you can go about 500 miles before refueling.

The systems are compact, efficient, and low maintenance. The interior has zebra wood cabinets, a teak countertop, cork, and hammered copper walls, and a Baltic birch ceiling with box-joint cedar shelving.

The side and rear windows, combined with the roof wall windows, keep it bright and spacious. With the awnings and screen room extended, a long-term base camp can be easily set up. Cooking can be done either inside or out.

There is a single-burner cooktop built into the teak countertop, and the dropdown table on the inside rear door holds another compact propane stove. Under the bench seat/bed is a 35-liter solar-powered, pull-out fridge.

Come bedtime, the bench seat turns into a bed, and the wall cushion rests on the removable redwood tabletop (stored under the bench seat) that is supported by three plywood legs that magnetically attach to the extended lower drawer guides. Takes a minute to set up.

In the upper nose cone is a pull-out bed —48″ × 84″—that rolls out on 300 pound drawer guides. This pull out is also the main storage area when driving—mostly sleeping bags and clothes.

The food and kitchenware are kept in a pair of drawers under the bench seat. On the passenger side of the cabin is a countertop with stove and sink, two drawers for cutlery and small personal items, and a smaller bench seat with an 18-gallon water tank underneath.

The cabin is small (25 sq. ft.) but feels spacious. and there is ample room for two adults to hang out and relax even in the worst weather. If the weather gets cold, there is a gasoline-fired air heater.

Dimmable LED rope lighting is concealed behind a cedar valance. Hot showers are done outdoors with a portable propane water heater. The one thing we don't carry most of the time is a cassette toilet. We have one, but if we are out camping, we find ways to do it outside the vehicle.

VITAL STATISTICS

- **Vehicle:** 2007 Jeep Wrangler Rubicon Unlimited — Earthroamer model: XV-JP #003

- **Rear cabin:** Balsa core fiberglass sandwich construction

- **Motor:** Standard 205 hp, 3.8L V6 gasoline; 12.5 mpg.

- **Sleeping:** Two down below, two in "nose cone" pull-out bed on 300 lb. drawer slides

- **2- or 4-wheel drive:** 4WD / automatic transmission / air lockers / sway bar disconnect

- **Suspension modification:** Nth Degree Suspension / 3.5″ front spring / 4.5″ rear springs / 5.13 gearing / Superchips Trail-Dash Performance Tuner / Earthroamer skid plates / LongRanger supplemental fuel tank that provides 40 gal. total fuel storage (500+ mi. range)

- **Water:** 18 gal. fresh water / stainless steel sink in teak countertop with faucet and water filter / water pump on spring-wound timer / outside cold water shower in propane locker

- **Cooking, Refrigerator:** Princess single-burner propane stove / 2.5 lb. propane tank in outside propane locker / 35L Dometic slide-out fridge / drop-down cooking table on inside of rear door

- **Awnings:** *Driver side:* Foxwing 270-degree awning. *Passenger side:* ARB 8′ × 8′ awning with zip-on screen room

- **Camping chairs, tables:** Redwood dining table with screw-on legs (table doubles as part of the lower sleeping platform) / Pico folding chairs

- **Jumper cables, tow ropes, tire pumps, traction pads:** Jumper cables (stored in side mount spare tire) / AEV front bumper with Warn 9.0 R.C. winch / Viair 88P portable compressor / Maxtrax traction pads (mount on engine compartment hood) / Hi-Lift jack / shovel / axe

- **Solar Panels:** Renogy 100-watt solar panel / Morningstar solar controller / Two 105Ah AGM batteries / Xantrex Prosine 1800W inverter / Xantrex charge controller

- **Air Heater:** Espar 7,500 BTU gasoline-fired

- **Ventilation Fan:** 3-speed Dometic Fan-Tastic fan

- **Shower, water heater:** Zodi propane-fired portable

- **Dometic dual-pane rear window** with built-in screen and privacy shade

- **AlumaBox storage** on outside of rear door

- **Rhino** roof rack

- **Firetruck steps** to access roof

- **50 ft. Heise** off-road LED front light bar

- **HID driving** lights

- **Audio, nav, and alarm systems**

"The side and rear windows, combined with the roof wall windows, keep it bright and spacious."

More...

"The cabin is small (25 sq. ft.), but feels spacious and there is ample room for two adults to hang out and relax."

XV-JP #03 gets a lot of attention. Almost everywhere we go, at every stop, people come over and want to know what it is. It's predictable that when the rear door opens and they see inside, their jaws drop and there is a half minute of silence while they process what they're seeing. It's fun sharing the story and hopefully providing some inspiration.

pauljensencustom.blogspot.com
www.hollowsurfboards.com
www.earthroamer.com

"It's fun sharing the story and hopefully providing some inspiration."

Foster's 1994 Toyota Land Cruiser

Foster Huntington

*F*OSTER HUNTINGTON WEARS MANY hats. *Photographer/builder/filmmaker/ designer/author/traveler/communicator/ surfer/skateboarder....*

In 2010, Foster had been working for a year as a menswear designer for Ralph Lauren in New York, when he decided to abandon the prestigious job for life on the road.

He had a blog called The Burning House, *where he asked: "If your house was burning, what would you take with you?" People sent in photos and lists and it got so popular that HarperCollins gave him a big advance to do a book called* The Burning House.

With the proceeds, he bought a 1987 VW Vanagon Syncro that had been well maintained by the previous owner (for $15,000), and in 2011 set out on road trips up and down the California coast, including a lot of time in Baja California, and up into the Sierras. He was 23.

On the road, he met other van dwellers, coined the hashtag "vanlife," and started posting on social media, first with a blog called The Restless Transplant, *then on Instagram (where he now has about a million followers).*

He stopped posting on the blog some years ago and now posts sparingly (mostly stories) on Instagram. His main focus these days is working in a movie studio that he and friends built next to his tree houses in Washington. (See The New York Times *feature article on him at:* **shltr.net/foster**.)

He's published several books, including Off Grid Life, Van Life, Home Is Where You Park It, *and* The Burning House: What People Would Take If the House Was on Fire.

I've been up to visit him twice in Washington, and he's come down here several times, and it's always inspiring to see what he's up to. In spite of our age difference, we both like to play and have daily adventures.

We've gone swimming in rivers on hot summer days, had wild duck dinners at Louie Frazier's riverside home in Mendocino County (riding a 500-foot zip line to get there), explored dark nights illuminated with his night vision goggles, and I've spent nights in each of his tree houses in Washington.

We covered his Tacoma Camper truck in Tiny Homes on the Move *in 2014. Since then he switched first to a Sprinter van, then more recently to the vehicle shown here.*

In the last few years, there's been an obvious surge in van (and other nomadic) living, and since Foster got into it early on, I thought it would be good to get his perspective on various modes of nomadic transport. I asked him to compare the four traveling homes he's owned in the last ten years. Here I've summarized his answers: —LK

1. He said the 1987 VW Vanagon Syncro was well suited for off-road travel, but that there were constant mechanical problems over the course of his two years and 70,000 miles. He says people often put larger engines in VW vans and end up blowing up transmissions.

2. The Toyota Tacoma with camper shell *(see pp. 22–23,* Tiny Homes on the Move*)*, as with all Tacomas, is a reliable off-road vehicle, but that to make it livable, his camper shell and accessories ended up weighing 2,000 pounds, while the half-ton Tacoma payload was 1,200 pounds. Too heavy with three people, 30 gallons of water, etc.

3. He had an early Sprinter van (actually a Dodge, but manufactured by Mercedes), 2-wheel drive, with a 118-inch wheelbase.* Wheelbases of current Sprinters are 128″, 144″, and 170″.

———
*Wheelbase: *Distance between front and rear axles*

The Sprinter (or Ford Transit, etc.) is basically a little house on wheels. It starts off being a house, whereas the Tacoma's strength is its off-road capability.

He says these larger vehicles are not very good at off-road travel; they're too long. The 4-wheel drives are bad with rugged or rutted travel; due to their unibody frameworks, they don't twist when a wheel hits a hole in rough terrain (like a Tacoma will) and the entire vehicle will tilt back and forth.

He found his Sprinter was great at long distance (on pavement) road trips.

In retrospect, the Tacoma excels at off-road travel, while a Sprinter's best feature is its livability.

4. He settled on the 1994 Toyota Land Cruiser shown here because it has a box frame (whereas Tacomas have channel frames), and it will carry a lot more weight than a Tacoma. It's great off road and it's easy to get parts for it. This is a well thought-out and constructed rig, as you can see from the photos and statistics.

He said if he were to build a rig now, it'd be a turbo diesel truck with cooking inside (cooking is outside with the Land Cruiser), and a stand-up pop-top.

Great sites for details on Foster's previous lives (including a lot on the Syncro):

 **www.arestlesstransplant.com instagram.com/fosterhunting**

VITAL STATISTICS

- **Vehicle:** 1994 Toyota Land Cruiser FZJ80
- **Motor:** 4.5L incline 6-cylinder
- **Transmission:** 4-speed automatic; full-time 4-wheel drive; 2-speed transfer
- **Suspension:** OME 2.5″ heavy lift
- **Fuel:** 38-gal. Long Range Australia tank
- **Range:** 500 mi.
- **Custom rear:** Built with 80-20 T-slot custom aluminum building system
- **Refrigerator:** Dometec 35L
- **Battery:** 12V isolated 50Ah lithium polymer battery pack (like a giant laptop battery)
- **Front bumper:** ARB bumper and Warn winch with synthetic line
- **Rear bumper:** 4×4 LABS with dual swing arms
- **Air compressor:** ARB high-output on-board air compressor with 5-gal. tank
- **Awning:** Alu-Cab 270° shadow awning (about $1,500 — opens in seconds)
- **Rooftop tent:** Alu-Cab 3.1 Expedition Tent (about $4,000)
- **Seats:** Scheel-Mann heated seats
- **Stove:** Tembotusk Skottle
- **Rear window:** Emu Gull Wing
- **Recovery gear:** Maxtrax recovery boards

"It's great off road and it's easy to get parts for it."

If you're considering a rig, he says three important things to ask are:
- Where do you want to go?
- How long will you be on the road?
- Do you need 4-wheel drive?

More...

"It has a box frame ... and it will carry a lot more weight than a Tacoma."

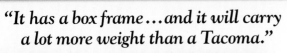

1992 Land Rover Defender

Oso Steen and Marcus Whitaker

I've known the extraordinarily talented Steen family for almost 20 years now: Bill, Athena, and their sons Benito, Oso, and Kalin.

Our lives have entwined over that period, and even before, when Bill and Athena were inspired by a photograph of a Nebraska barn with straw bale walls in our book Shelter *(page 70).*

They went on to write the best-selling book, The Straw Bale House *in 1994, a forerunner for the straw bale building movement, and their work has been featured in our books* Home Work, Tiny Homes, *and* Small Homes.

They live on a 40-acre homestead in the Arizona desert, where they have a complex of beautiful straw bale buildings and teach classes in natural building: **www.caneloproject.com**

Bill and I are both lifelong photographers and lately have been talking on the phone about the amazing photographic capabilities of iPhones.

The other day, I told Bill we were about to wrap up production of this book, and he mentioned that his son Oso and a friend had refurbished and kitted out a 1994 Land Rover. I got in touch with Oso, who sent me the photos and story of this remarkable vehicle.

Here is Oso's partner, Marcus Whittaker, describing the building process.

–LK

L-R: Marcus, Ray, Oso, Kalin

THE BUILD STARTED IN AUGUST, 2020, when Ray Tien commissioned an extensive truck restoration and camper, with Oso taking the lead on the camper build and the Land Rover itself being restored and upgraded in the UK prior to export.

Ray wanted this to be both an extremely capable on- and off-road vehicle with homey comfort inside — a place where Ray and his wife Caroline could go to Canada and even Alaska in the winter for back country skiing, but also head down to Baja and beyond in the summer time. He wanted to have the ability to cruise on the highway all day and then hit the mountains or beach to camp in the evening — day after day.

The chassis was completely restored and strengthened in the rear, the engine was torn down and rebuilt, the suspension upgraded, with locking differentials front and back, and a big old turbo installed to crank up the power to cope with American highways.

The really exciting part for us was Ray's trust, appreciation for Oso's craft, and willingness to follow our suggestions and ideas to make the build work.

As much as the skill and dedication of the team who worked on this truck, Ray's cool, calm, and encouraging attitude throughout the build held the project together and allowed everyone to do their best work.

Building a home in the roughly 30-square-foot back of a Land Rover Defender is a challenge to say the least.

The Alu Cab (a South African overland vehicle outfitting company) Icarus rooftop conversion was the starting point, with over seven feet of head room when popped up and a bed the entire nine-foot length of the roof.

With room up top for bedding and some clothes, there is still enough room downstairs for a lounging area that converts to a full bed, a kitchen with custom-fabricated, stainless steel fridge, sink, slide-out mesquite office desk, and storage for clothes and gear.

There is a 2000-watt inverter for powering electronics and heat via the Espar diesel heater. The idea is for Ray and Caroline to be able to travel and enjoy adventures in this truck, but also to hunker down and work when needed.

The defining feature of this build is the slide-out kitchen. A stainless steel box mounted to the chassis has a 500 lb. capacity slideout supporting a nested array of features: a sink connected to the

"Ray wanted this to be both an extremely capable on- and off-road vehicle with homey comfort inside."

chassis-mounted, 16-gallon water tank, a dual-burner, Partner Steel propane stove, quick-connected to another chassis-mounted propane tank, and a lovely thick mesquite work top, hidden cutting board, and storage drawers to house cooking and eating ware.

It took several tries to get this design right, and it turned out to be an elegant and functional outdoor cooking space — quick to set up and enjoyable to use.

It is worth noting that all the mesquite and ash in this build was harvested by Oso in Canelo, Arizona, and the lumber milled and dried onsite. The work is exacting and exquisite with details such as the mesquite bow ties on the ash fridge door — being as enjoyable to look at as the mountain and desert scenery outside.

 *www.caneloproject.com*

More...

"The idea is for Ray and Caroline to be able to travel and enjoy adventures in this truck but also to hunker down and work when needed."

VITAL STATISTICS

- **Vehicle:** 1992 Land Rover Defender 110
- **Engine:** 200 Tdi rebuilt
- **Gearbox:** Rebuilt R380 5-speed gearbox from Ashcroft transmissions
- **Transfer case:** Rebuilt LT230 1.4 transfer case
- **Turbo:** Garret Variable Geometry turbocharger
- **Tires:** Cooper STT Pro 285 75 r16 MT
- **Suspension:** 3 in. lift / Adrenaline 4×4 cranked radius and control arms
- **Shocks:** Old Man Emu BP51 bypass reservoir shock absorbers
- **Springs:** Old man Emu HD front springs / Eibach 2 in. lift rear springs with Gwynn Lewis leveling spacers to lift one side

- **Water:** 60L water tank
- **Space heating:** Espar D2 Airtronic diesel heater
- **Interior stove:** Eno single-burner stove
- **Exterior stove:** Cook Partner two-burner stove
- **Sinks:** Exterior and interior
- **Solar:** Two 120W CMP walk-on solar panels
- **Batteries:** Two 100Ah Discover Lithium Blue deep-cycle batteries
- Victron 1200W inverter / Victron 30A charge controller / Victron 30A DC–DC charger / Victron AC–DC charger
- **Hot water:** Falcon tank heater

- **Propane:** 2.4 gal. aluminum propane tank
- **Water pump:** Shurflo Aqua King II
- **Interior wood:** Mesquite countertops / Arizona Ash cabinetry
- **Refrigerator:** 60L custom fridge with Isotherm remote compressor
- **Rooftop sleeping:** Alu-Cab Icarus Rooftop Conversion
- **Shade:** Alu-Cab Shadow Awning
- **Air compressor:** ARB front and rear lockers actuated by a twin-motor high-flow ARB compressor
- **Winch:** Red Winch Explorer 2 (10,000 lbs.)

"Building a home in the roughly 30-square-foot back of a Land Rover Defender is a challenge to say the least."

"The defining feature of this build is the slide-out kitchen."

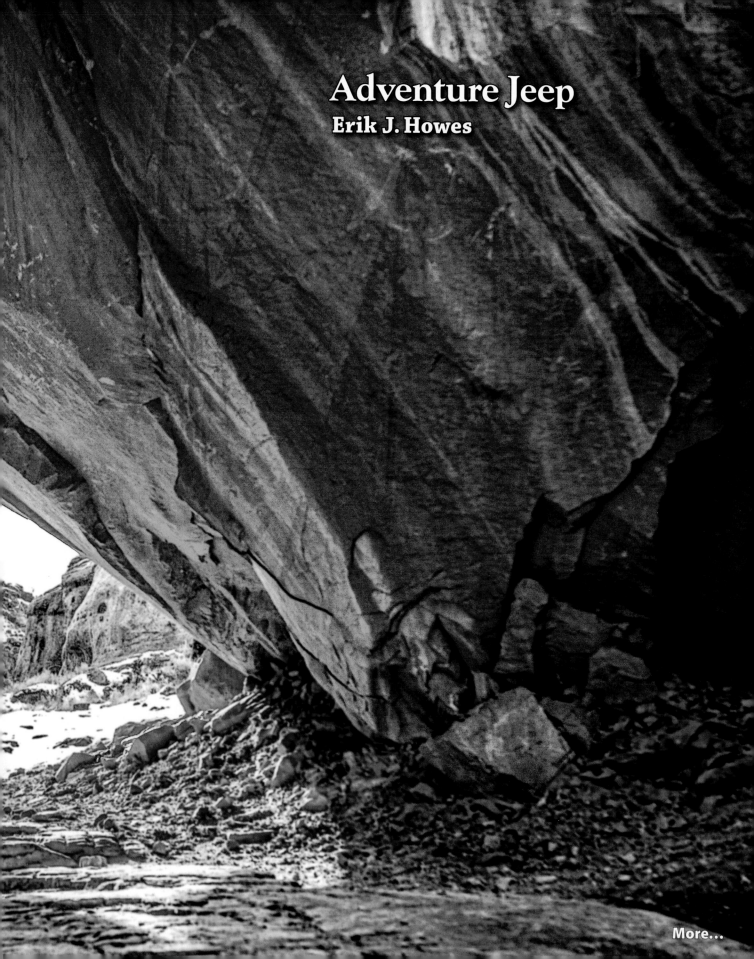

Adventure Jeep

Erik J. Howes

More…

SEVEN YEARS AGO, I WAS WORKING 50+ hour weeks as a mechanic at the local Jeep dealership in my hometown. You could find me either smoking unfiltered cigarettes or turning wrenches with grease up to my elbows. This life was wearing out my body, and even more so, my mind.

That was the year I found rock climbing, and it was the year I bought the Jeep. Back then it had a leaky fold-down canvas top, and I was naïve about what living a life on the road would be like.

I packed up to travel in that tent-on-wheels for what was supposed to be only a few months of driving cross country to go rock climbing and to experience all the places I'd seen only in books.

Before I left, I sold my mechanic's tools — a way to solidify my decision to leave the trade. I didn't want to come back from that trip and continue being the same person. That money allowed me to travel the country, but in reality, it allowed me to start a new life.

It's been quite a few years since that first road trip. Since then, both of us have changed quite a bit. I slowly built the soft top from the inside out, installing an over-the-wheel-well kitchen counter and built-in dashboard cabinets. Then one cold winter, I replaced the top itself with the cedar shake micro-house you see here.

It's built almost entirely of scrap and salvaged materials I found. The metal roof is from an old farmhouse; the flashing is made of chimney pipes and is framed with offcuts from a barn build's scrap pile. The only things purchased were some tubes of adhesive to keep the shingles fixed and some fresh roofing screws with gaskets to keep the metal down and leakproof.

Every season starts with a power wash to get the cedar clean, and a week or so of fixes and upgrades to make the space as comfortable as can be. This little adventure mobile is constantly evolving, as I do with it. It's been amazing to look through old pictures for this Shelter Publications project and to see how far we have come. To think, it all started with that first road trip.

VITAL STATISTICS

- **Vehicle:** 2002 Jeep Wrangler TJ 4.0L
- **Transmission:** 5-speed manual
- **Mileage:** 195,000 mi.
- **Insulation:** 2″ rigid foam board & spray foam
- **Heater:** Webasto Air Top 2000 gasoline heater
- **Electricity:** Goal Zero Yeti 400 battery-powered portable power station
- **Bed:** Salvaged styrofoam, scrap yoga mats & army surplus blanket
- **Stove:** MSR Pocket Rocket

What info can you pass along to people building or outfitting a vehicle?

Very rarely does life align to make converting a vehicle a "convenient" thing to do. The process is almost always bumpy, and pursuing a project like this takes energy, time, and sacrifices. It will almost certainly be uncomfortable or scary. But learning to breathe through the process and taking breaks when needed can make the journey much easier.

Don't be limited by what you think a conversion "should be." Follow your creative vision. But also be realistic about your ability and don't build something that will fall off on the highway or get rattled loose on washboard roads.

Make sure to build something that can withstand hurricane-force winds and an earthquake. Triangles are strong; squares, not so much.

What would you do differently if you had it to do over again?

Start with a bigger vehicle. A 20-square-foot vehicle with a bed only one inch longer than you is a tight living space. I have spent well over 1,000 nights inside here and if things were, say, 20% bigger, I probably wouldn't have this persistent kink in my shoulder.

 instagram.com/smellybagofdirt
instagram.com/squallythetrolley
www.staywildnevermild.com

> *"It's built almost entirely of scrap and salvaged materials I found."*

*"This little adventure mobile
is constantly evolving, as I do with it."*

59

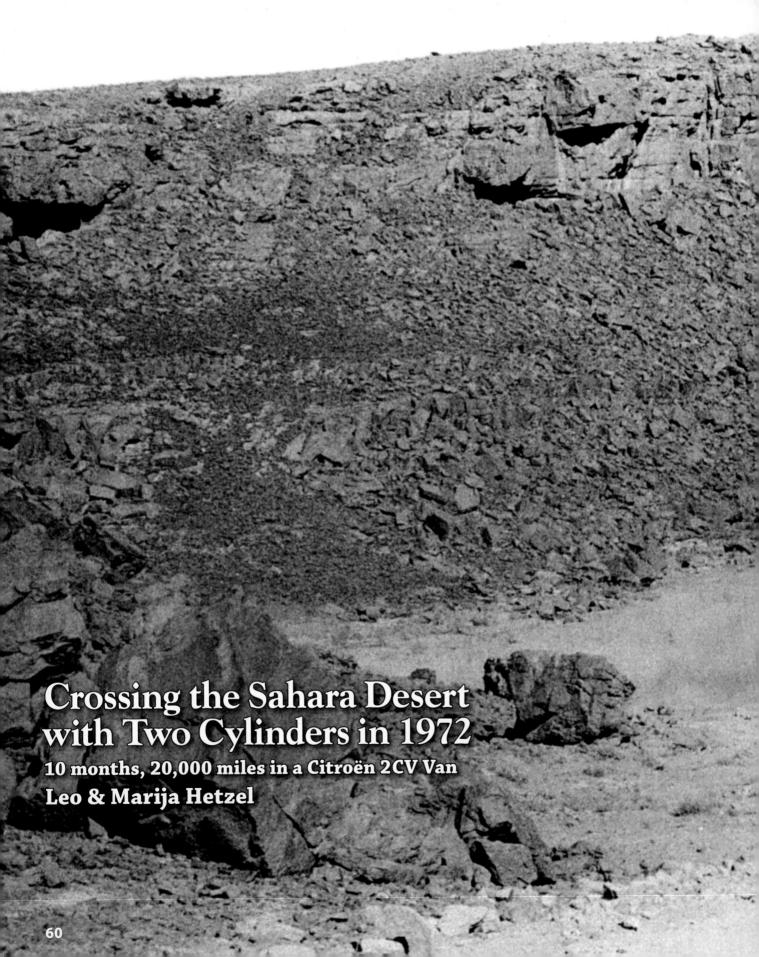

Crossing the Sahara Desert with Two Cylinders in 1972

10 months, 20,000 miles in a Citroën 2CV Van

Leo & Marija Hetzel

More…

Algeria, Sahara Desert. Citroën between In Amenas and Djanet

"We found the cheapest option was a new Citroën 2CV (two-cylinder) van, which we bought from the factory in Paris for $1,500."

I met Leo in the water 15 years ago. Two old guys on long boards, surfing at San Juanico (Scorpion Bay) in Baja California.

I was traveling in my 1978 Tacoma with rooftop tent, and Leo and family had set up a substantial beachside camp, all of which came out of a meticulously packed Isuzu Trooper.

Turned out we had a lot in common. Surfing, photography, camping, Baja, adventuring....

Leo was a well-known surfing photographer for many years, and when we met, he was working as staff photographer for the Long Beach Press-Telegram.

He had told me about his trip through the Sahara in the '70s, so when we started putting this book together, I got in touch. An amazing journey, with beautiful photos, covering 20,000 miles in a 36-horsepower $1600 Citroën 2CV, a unique, simple vehicle, much beloved by auto aficionados. (One can't help but compare this with today's $150,000 road rigs.)

—LK

(See pp. 68–69 for the Australian adventures of Leo's son Yasha in a later model Citroën van.)

IN 1972 MY WIFE MARIJA AND I WERE living in Europe when we got a letter from our French friends, Christianne and Daniel Boone, asking if we wanted to visit some prehistoric cave paintings on the Tassili Plateau in the middle of the Sahara Desert in Algeria. We decided to go for it.

In those days, most people with money crossed in Land Rovers and some in VW buses. But we found the cheapest option was a new Citroën 2CV (two-cylinder) van, which we bought at the factory in Paris for $1,500.

We headed to Palič, Yugoslavia to build a minimal camper with the help of Marija's carpenter father. We used all hand tools, except for a drill that I bought, and a welder borrowed for the roof rack.

We gathered basic cooking utensils, a foam rubber mattress, and a few other things. I had a little brass Primus stove, which a mountain climber friend in Peru had given me. It was perfect: small, light, and could run on regular gasoline.

In Algiers, Tunisia we found we needed more: extra tires, gas cans, water cans, and a sand ladder to help us across the dunes. We found some leaky metal jerry cans in a flea market that were probably left over from WWII. Luckily, they had been used for olive oil and didn't explode when we found a guy to weld them. From Algiers, we headed with Christianne and Daniel toward the cave paintings.

There's plenty to see in the Sahara and we weren't in a hurry, so we stopped in small towns and oases and met many interesting people.

To get to the cave paintings, we hired a Tuareg guide to lead us on a long hike up to the plateau where the paintings are. They are spectacular; some go back as far as 10,000 years — when the Sahara was much greener than it is now.

Sahara Desert. Leo and Marija at the end of a paved road in the Algerian Sahara. Now the fun starts.

Algeria, Sahara Desert. Citroën between In Amenas and Djanet. There were some places on the gravel, dust, and rock road that went up steep hills. If we didn't get a running start, the front drive of the Citroën would lose traction and we'd go back down and try again.

After visiting the paintings, our friends went back to France, and we continued across the desert alone in our little two-cylinder van. Looking back now, I'm amazed at what we did.

There are lots of little side roads and it was sometimes difficult to know which one was the main route. We heard stories of people that got lost and weren't found until it was too late.

There is one stretch between Tamanrasset, Algeria and Agadez, Niger that is 900 kilometers (560 miles) with nothing—no water, no gas, no oases, no people. I think it took us three days to go those 900 kilometers.

We got stuck a lot and had dozens of flat tires caused by bushes with big thorns like nails. The tires on the van were tubeless, but we put tubes in them and carried extras. In Algiers, we bought a big rubber hammer, two big tire pry bars, and a hand air pump. We'd break the tire away from the rim, patch the tube, put it back together, and pump it up with the hand pump.

It was very hot, so Marija would take a little towel and wet it to cool herself off. It would dry out in five or ten minutes.

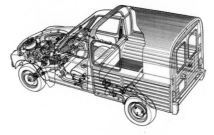

We carried four five-gallon metal jerry cans full of gas and about 10 gallons of water, plus two extra spare tires and all our living stuff. It was a lot of extra weight, most of which was in the middle of the van. The Citroën doesn't have a regular frame like a normal car or truck; the body is on a belly pan that runs the length of the van, the same as the old VW bugs. The constant banging and

bouncing around on bad roads caused the van to bend in the middle.

After a temporary fix, we finally made it to Agadez, Niger, which is a special place marking the southern edge of the Sahara. It's one of the main jumping-off places for the camel caravans going north across the Sahara and where the caravans first stop when they are coming south.

In post-war Nigeria, everyone told us that we should never pull over on the side of the road to sleep because there were former soldiers still running around with guns, robbing and killing people. Instead, the villagers always invited us into their compounds to sleep safely.

Near Lake Chad is a town that was one of our favorites in all of West Africa: Maiduguri, a very traditional Muslim place. Back then there were very few tourists up in the far north, and today there are almost none because of the terrorist group Boko Haram.

We were always respected and treated well in the Islamic parts of North and West Africa. It makes me sad that we will never be able to go back in our lifetime.

We made it to Lake Chad, but the lake was fast disappearing because of the dams in the rivers that feed the lake. It will probably be totally gone some day and the people that depend on it will have to go somewhere else.

After that, we headed for the coast. In the town of Abomey, in what is now Benin, people said we needed to photograph the King of Abomey. They said he was 117 years old and had 27 wives, but I only saw one of them and 117 was a bit of a stretch.

We went north into a primitive area where the tribes worship mud idols and have wonderful little castles built out of mud and dirt.

In Senegal, I saw good waves but didn't have a surfboard, so I did some body surfing.

More...

CROSSING THE SAHARA

We wanted to get to Timbuktu but were stopped by a flooding Niger River. Then we tried to drive to Senegal, but the road was so bad we had to turn back and put the Citroën on a train.

I wanted to drive back across the Sahara through Mauritania to Morocco, but Marija was more sensible. When I look back, I think she was right; it could have been a very sketchy, dangerous trip.

So, from Senegal, we put our Citroën on a ship to the Canary Islands and from there back to Spain and Granada, where we spent time in the caves and enjoyed some good flamenco music and Spanish wine with our gypsy friends. Then we returned to Marija's hometown in Yugoslavia to re-weld our bent Citroën so we could sell it.

I wasn't getting freelance photography jobs or selling many photographs, so it was time to go back home to California after a seven-year adventure with my new wife and get a job and have a couple of kids and buy a house and live the American dream. We've always wanted to get back to the Sahara Desert, but it's never happened.

We both miss our dependable little Citroën. It took us on an adventure of a lifetime and never failed us. Back in California, a friend gave us the next best thing: a 1957 VW bus that had been a taxi in Tijuana, Mexico, and it took us on many adventures in the decades after.

instagram.com/fotohetzel
archiv-e.com/collections/leo-hetzel

Cameras: 2 Nikon F's
Film: Kodak Ektachrome 64 ASA (ISO); Kodak Tri-X

I think that when people think about the Sahara Desert, they think of sand and sand dunes. The Sahara is much more than just sand dunes. There are mountains and rocks and gravel and, in some spots, sparse vegetation. These dunes are in eastern Algeria bordering with Libya, near In Amenas. They are huge, almost sand mountains, and they move. There are small villages in some parts of the Sahara that the dunes cover and the villagers must move. Sometimes, years later, the villages reappear and people move back into them.

Our Citroën crossing the Doué River to get to Podor, which is on the border between Senegal and Mauritania.

Fulani man. West Africa, Sahara Desert, Upper Volta, now called Burkina Faso, in and around a town named Dori. The people are Bella and Fulani.

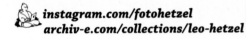

Bamako, Mali, West Africa. Our Citroën on the train from Bamako to Senegal. We tried to drive to Senegal from Mali, but the road was impassable, so we put the car on a train to Senegal.

Somba man in northwestern Benin (formerly the Kingdom of Dahomey), near Natitingou

Ghana, West Africa. Marija cooking in Citroën with kids watching

Mali, West Africa. Kids can make toys out of anything.

Niger, Fulani man. One day when we stopped to make lunch, this Fulani man arrived and sat down under the tree and watched make lunch. We hadn't passed a village or seen anyone for several hours and he just appeared. We offered him water and eventually he disappeared back into the desert.

Senegal, West Africa, near Saint-Louis. Marija making Turkish coffee

More...

Young Fulani man. West Africa, Sahara Desert, Upper Volta, now called Burkina Faso, in and around a town named Dori. The people are Bella and Fulani.

Ghana, West Africa, Dixcove and Princes Town. Waves in Dixcove Another good point break and no board to ride the waves

Bella woman. West Africa, Sahara Desert, Upper Volta, now called Burkina Faso, in and around a town named Dori. The people are Bella and Fulani.

Guitar player and singer from the Babur tribe in northern Nigeria, near Maiduguri. When we were traveling in Nigeria, everyone told us not to just park on the side of the road and sleep. It was not many years after the Biafra war and there were still armed men running around and robbing people. One evening, as we were looking for a village to sleep in, we arrived at a village and this man said that we could park our car in front of his compound. We cooked dinner, and when it was dark, got in the car to sleep. A little later we heard the most beautiful music, so we got out of the car and sat with the villagers as our host played and sang. The music was out of this world. The next morning I asked if I could take a picture of him and his family. He put on his best clothes and I got my picture. This picture brings back wonderful memories of that night and the music.

Hausa Village, Niger

Woman in market in Azare,
in northern Nigeria

Nigeria, north. Hausa village

Upper Volta, now called Burkina Faso,
in the market of the town Dori.

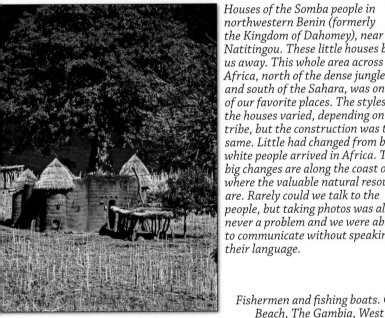

Houses of the Somba people in
northwestern Benin (formerly
the Kingdom of Dahomey), near
Natitingou. These little houses blew
us away. This whole area across West
Africa, north of the dense jungle
and south of the Sahara, was one
of our favorite places. The styles of
the houses varied, depending on the
tribe, but the construction was the
same. Little had changed from before
white people arrived in Africa. The
big changes are along the coast or
where the valuable natural resources
are. Rarely could we talk to the
people, but taking photos was almost
never a problem and we were able
to communicate without speaking
their language.

Niger. After crossing the main part of the Sahara, the
first country we came to was Niger. This was a well
where the Fulani were drawing water for their cattle.
While I shot photos, several of the Fulani came over to
the car to talk to Marija.

Fishermen and fishing boats. Gunjur
Beach, The Gambia, West Africa

Nigeria, Kano. Wherever we parked,
there was usually a crowd.

Second Generation Citroën

Yasha Hetzel

(See the previous eight pages on the Citroën trip in the Sahara taken by Yasha's mom and dad in 1972.)

THIS WAS A 2001 CITROËN BERLINGO that I bought for $6,000 when I started studying for my Ph.D. in Perth. I had been looking for a Camry station wagon when I stumbled on this ex-caterer's van and realized this was the new version of the van that had taken my parents across the Sahara before I was born.

I had heard all the stories, so when I found this van, my imagination went wild thinking of all the adventures I could have. The van came through with the goods too, and took me across Australia twice, and up to the North West *(these photos)* dozens of times over seven years.

I added more than 200,000 kilometers to the odometer and never broke down on the thousands of kilometers of corrugated roads on the way to remote surf spots. I built a bed in the back, with plastic boxes underneath to store food, wetsuits, and camping gear; I never removed these, so I was always ready for weekend getaways.

The first photo below is of one of those swell runs up north, after a 14-hour drive and a few hours sleep in the car park, awakened by the rumble of a new swell.

I rigged up a bungee cord system in the ceiling from which I could hang four boards above the bed and sleep without moving anything around.

The 1.4-liter engine was super economical (good for a student), and since it was built to transport pallets (of baguettes, I presume). I could load it up as much as I liked and never suffer bad fuel economy. The light truck tires were tough too, so I never had a flat.

Corrado, the Italian mechanic that kept it running smoothly, would happily slot it in between the Audis and BMWs, and endearingly called it "The Beast." My friends called it "the bread van," never wasting an opportunity to question my masculinity as I parked between all the rugged Land Cruisers — but the fact that I was parked between the 4×4s meant I never had to do much to defend its virtues.

Eventually, after I got my Ph.D., I sold the van to a backpacker rental company for $1,200 with half a million kilometers on the odometer, still running perfectly. With a wife and a kid on the way, the lack of a back seat meant it was time to move on. Now I have proper 4-wheel drive which can go anywhere, but strangely enough, has yet to go a fraction of the places the Citroën did.

It took two days on the longest straight stretch of road in Australia to cross the Nullarbor Plain parallel to the cliffs (shown in photo at right). The dark skies and bright stars in the middle of the Nullarbor made for a memorable night camping in the Citroen.

> *"The van came through with the goods too, and took me across Australia twice, and up to the North West."*

"Now I have proper 4-wheel drive which can go anywhere, but strangely enough, has yet to go a fraction of the places the Citroën did."

The cliffs along the Great Australian Bight continue across the southern edge of the continent and once connected Australia to Antarctica.

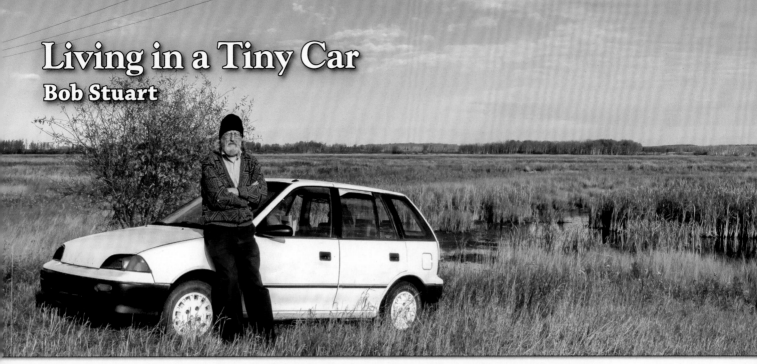

Living in a Tiny Car
Bob Stuart

"This one is built more for mileage than comfort, but it has all the facilities — indoors, if necessary — for storm or stealth."

About 20 years ago, my friend John Welles (who was 6´4´) used to spend a couple of winter months in Hawaii. It's a lot more difficult to pull off the road and camp in the Hawaiian Islands than it is, say, in California (or some place like Nevada).

John would rent a small car and rig up a mattress from the passenger seat back into the trunk, and when he was sleeping at night, it looked just like any parked car.

In recent years, with what is a huge interest in on-road living, vans have become the most popular vehicles. They are roomy, you can move from front to back inside the vehicle, and they are adaptable to infinite designs.

The idea of a very small car that can serve as a home and at the same time be unobtrusive is a completely different approach — lean and mean.

I'm amazed at what Bob has done here — the thoughtfulness of this design. He's thought of all kinds of things that would never occur to most people and has worked them out in his design and construction.

In fact, this is one of the most complex builds in this book. Everything is so tight that it's hard to show how everything is working together. If you study the drawing on page 73, it will give you an idea of the layout. This is a treasure trove of design considerations for the do-it-yourself stealth traveler. You just need to study it for a while.
—LK

THIS ONE IS BUILT MORE FOR MILEAGE than comfort, but it has all the facilities — indoors, if necessary — for storm or stealth.

I started my West Coast life with two months of bicycle camping. So later, when I was car-camping (in an '80 Toyota Celica liftback) to find my current house, I felt like I was wasting about half of a vast space, yet living awkwardly. After a few more iterations, I finally hit on what feels right.

One key was to stop trying to use the driver's seat and its on-road conveniences when parked. I keep only the driver's seat, which is sacrificed in camp to sitting sideways on the bed, which takes up the passenger side.

Kitchen chores are done while seated, and there is even an emergency baggie-toilet built into the seat. A plastic sheet allows a sponge bath, and the footwell holds enough water to rinse off shampoo.

The sink can drain either through the floor or into a tank, and it holds the utensils for drying and storage. The mesh overhead is for drying towels and clothes.

The car shown is a 3-cylinder Suzuki Swift, which was also sold under the GM name brand of Geo Metro from '88 thru '94. It is getting rare, but this layout should work for almost any small car, and usually better. With a car this short, I have to park uphill to get a level bed.

This is still a work in progress. The rear, multipurpose space could get another set of drawers, but I like the option of doing a full-length stretch.

The terrycloth drapes should be fastened at the bottom to catch condensation and wick it away, with a quick furling arrangement.

The whole rig fits in a similar two-door coupe I'm working on, with smoked rear windows. With a fake passenger headrest over the bed and no drapes, it will look unoccupied except for condensation.

With room in the fender for machinery, the can cooler could be replaced by a hacked refrigerator with freezer. At one cubic foot, it would have one inch of insulation, and all but the freezer could slide out for easy access.

The whole car should get serious insulation. I'd also like to install a tank with circulating water, mostly full of paraffin in thin plastic tubes to provide steady heat as the wax turns solid overnight. It could be re-melted by engine coolant, a water muffler, an evening fire (the fastest on-road option), or solar.

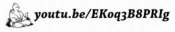 *youtu.be/EKoq3B8PRIg*

The shoe organizer attached to the back of the seat is handy for kitchen supplies and waste. The driver's footwell can be used for temporary storage and wet gear. Two-door access is easier, but this works.

The front drawers are handy while driving and in camp, and can store the bedding under the dash. The orange flash under the bed is a survival suit, stored as insulation.

There's a CO detector in the overhead mesh. Screens on the visored side windows work well for moderate conditions. The stepped cutting board borrows the forward stove mounting for travel.

The recliner position for the seat back, salvaged from an office chair. The utility cover under the sink is shown askew, and the drawers locked for travel. The front drawers can be suspended or moved to the countertop.

The boat is Lambordinghy, a Pygmy Kayaks Queen Charlotte 19 kit converted to stinkin' fast pedal power with a SpinFin (not mounted).

The foot-operated water pump, originally for an air mattress, and a handy under-seat tank to feed it. The space for a built-in slide-out refrigerator is currently occupied by a Peltier junction 6-pack cooler.

Counter space is about 2´×2´. Foreground is the gardener's pressure sprayer that rinses dishes with minimal water.

The stove travels out of the way, and can do simmering there. Also showing is the deep-cycle battery, and one of three inverters for various loads.

The cutting board is a two-level affair, so supplies can sit higher over my knees, and the chopped veggies easily funnel off against the riser.

My luxuries are a bread maker and a toaster. The water hose clips onto the top drawer to hit the sink.

Drawer detail, under construction. There is no wasted volume within the cabinet, but also no fancy joinery, just rectangular blocks glued to thin plywood.

Cabinet installed, sink open, drawer-locking bar on top. The sink drawer and the shallow drawer above it are short to provide room for the refrigerator, which can slide out into the footwell. Some drawer backs are modified to follow the wheel well. The panel covering the spare tire is undersize, so it can slide around for access to storage around the tire.

"This layout should work for almost any small car."

The seat cushion folds up, revealing the emergency toilet, which ziplocks onto the seat parts.

The seat bottom is adjustable to match the slope of the parking spot, with four settings. The baggie ziplocks onto the seat. Also showing are the sink drain hose and the battery charging cable (used as one conductor).

Seat set in low position. For toilet use, water bags are removed.

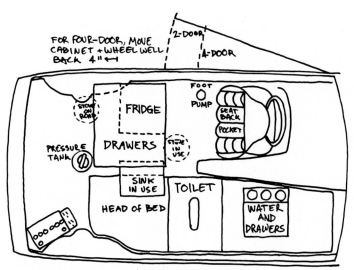

FOR FOUR-DOOR, MOVE CABINET + WHEEL WELL BACK 4" ←→

2-DOOR
4-DOOR

STOVE ON ROAD

FRIDGE

FOOT PUMP

SEAT BACK

POCKET

DRAWERS

STOVE IN USE

PRESSURE TANK

SINK IN USE

TOILET

HEAD OF BED

WATER AND DRAWERS

"This is still a work in progress."

Drawn to scale for the two-door coupe. I started with a scale drawing of the car, and sketched until I had the cabinet size. Then, a cardboard mockup confirmed it. Next came a full cutting list for the drawers and cabinet. Most of the material was scrounged. The battery and inverters were the most expensive bits by far.

Not full stealth, but inconspicuous. It could be raining, with cross-flow ventilation for the stove under the awnings on screened windows. One can slither from driving to camping without opening the door in places where mosquitoes would have hikers on the run, or back to driving for a hasty departure.

For Bob's Mom's VW Camper, see next page.

Mother Trucker

Bob Stuart

MY MOTHER SPENT THE WARM halves of her last 40 years mostly visiting parks. After having seen how she had been able to handle her Ford Cortina wagon and Holden station wagon, I realized that she was the only person I knew who could drive a VW bus without burning out the #3 exhaust valve, and I recommended one. By then, she was driving the Alaska Highway every other year, wintering near Toronto.

She had a very simple setup: no pop top, just a bench bed with boxes under it, and a small cabinet behind the passenger seat. When she visited me in Victoria, I added styrofoam insulation to her MK II model.

Two years later, she was about 62 degrees north, chatting with a young waitress at a truck stop. The girl admired her tidy little rig and asked what Mom would sell it for.

With nothing else to do that evening, Mom decided to teach the kid a lesson

in economics, and added up all the costs of a bus ticket back to Edmonton, hotel time, another VW, etc., for a grand total of $14,000.

The same waitress was there the next morning, and Mom gave her the sad news.

The kid just reached into her apron pocket and started peeling hundreds off a roll. Two hours later, Mom was sitting there with two cardboard boxes, a bus ticket, and slow service.

Ruth Stuart, 1917–2005. She had Asperger's, but mildly enough that she thought everyone else was off-kilter. I once wrote her that I'd seen a bumper sticker reading "Mother Trucker," and she just had to have one. I finally bought her the individual letters, and then realized that there was a culture clash set to go off. Sure enough, that summer a young couple walking by her campsite called out "Love your slogan!"

"Go away! I'm reading!" replied mother.

—Bob Stuart, Saskatchewan, Canada

El Burro – Overland Pack Mule

Jamie Wiseman

"I set out to build a one-of-a-kind, adventurous but utilitarian VW Beetle."

MY WIFE AND I PURCHASED A 1967 VW bug in August 2017 as a restoration project to flip and sell. We had a road trip to Colorado planned for June 2018 to camp and see the back country. We thought it would be cool to take a Baja bug out west on a outdoor adventure.

So I started to look at Baja kits and other off-road VW Beetles, but nothing looked looked like what we wanted. Then one day I was watching a video on YouTube about overlanding and it hit me!

We needed to build the bug like an overland vehicle. I set out to build a one-of-a-kind, adventurous but utilitarian VW Beetle.

I built (fabricated) everything myself.

Model made by Sharon Tarshish (shltr.net/tarshish)

"We needed to build the bug like an overland vehicle."

VITAL STATISTICS

Car

- 1.5″ tube bumpers front and rear
- Warn 5,000 lb. winch mounted to front bumper
- Custom roof rack to hold spare tire and two 4.5-gal. RotopaX fuel cans, jack, and traction mats
- Engine is a VW Type 1, fully modified dual port that is bored and stroked to 2234cc, using a AS21 late-model VW case and CB Performance Panchito 044 cylinder heads.
- Holly Sniper–equipped fuel injection system
- It puts out over 150 hp.
- *Fuel mileage:* 16–18 mpg on the highway and around 14–16 mpg towing the trailer; pretty good considering the vehicle weighs about 3,000 lbs.
- Suspension was modified for a 4″ wider stance, it has a completely custom-fabricated front A-arm suspension with FOA Coilover shocks giving it a lift of 4″.
- Rear suspension is also modified with rear trailing arms that are 2″ longer and 2″ wider, and equipped with FOA rear shocks and Sway-A-Way brand rear axles with Porsche CV joints.
- 3″ body lift to give it some fender clearance
- 002 VW Bus Transaxle built by Benco Racing. It is geared low with a 5.375 final drive, so first gear is made for low speed and crawling over terrain.
- Heavy-duty steering rack and pinion and electric power steering designed for a Polaris RZR UTV
- Power steering was a great addition since it has to turn the 30 × 9.5–15 tires.
- *Tires:* General Grabbers A/T on the front, 31 × 10.5–15 Grabbers on the rear, giving it some more flotation and traction
- To cool things down when it's hot I installed a custom-built A/C system using a Subaru Outback compressor, and for warmth it has a Webasto diesel-fueled parking heater.
- The dash houses all the gauges and A/C vents and sound system.
- The interior is fully soundproof and carpeted.
- Seats are out of a 2004 Honda Civic and reupholstered.
- For safety and to make the car more rigid, we fabricated a 10-point roll cage that ties everything together.
- The roll cage was good because I ended up building an off-road trailer to tow behind the Burro. So the roll cage tied into the rear bumper, giving it strength.

"It puts out over 150 hp."

More…

Trailer

Our off-road trailer build was a great addition to the Burro. It's built completely out of angle steel to help with the weight. We mounted a CVT Rainier tent on the top.

- Inside is storage for clothing and supplies, the Dometic CFX45 fridge, a two-burner cooktop, and a pantry.
- To stay clean on the trail we installed a Road Shower.
- Everything is powered by one Renology 100W solar panel and a deep-cycle battery.

I had to make the trailer match the Burro, so it was sprayed with the same Desert Tan paint, and I installed some VW taillights to match. The total weight of the trailer fully loaded is about 1,500 lbs., and the Burro has no problem pulling it at 60–65 mph.

It took about nine months to complete El Burro and it's an ongoing project. The trailer took about six months.

 www.instagram.com/jamiewiseman

"Everything is powered by one Renology 100-watt solar panel and a deep-cycle battery."

*"It's an
ongoing project."*

SunRay's Solar Electric Diesel Hybrid Vardo

SunRay Kelley

Photos by Roxanne Wilbur

SUNRAY KELLEY, FEATURED IN OUR BOOK Builders of the Pacific Coast, *continues his unique series of designs with this extraordinary vehicle that runs on sunlight.*

In collaboration with Bret and Kira Belan of Solarrolla Electric Drive Vehicles* in Ashland, Oregon, SunRay converted this gas-powered vehicle into a solar electric diesel hybrid. Eighteen solar panels charge 42 Nissan Leaf batteries, which power a large electric motor.

When the battery bank runs low, the 4-cylinder diesel generator kicks in to power the electric motor and extend the vehicle's range. (This diesel/electric motor combination is called a "genset.")

This cedar-sided caravan has a 1937 Willys front end and SunRay's custom-made doors and grill. The curved window above the cab and the skylight over the bed are signature SunRay Kelley sculptural elements that let in a lot of sunlight and view.

The solar panels on the side open up and are adjustable for maximum solar exposure.

When the batteries are fully charged, the solar input is used to heat water.

For inquiries about this vehicle (it's for sale) or to commission a custom conversion of your own, email **sunray@sunraykelley.com**.

–LK

 www.solarrolla.com

"When the battery bank runs low, the 4-cylinder diesel generator kicks in to power the electric motor."

"The solar panels on the side open up and are adjustable for maximum solar exposure."

Solar-Powered Electric Vans

Brett and Kira Belan

Photos (unless otherwise noted) by Kira Belan

Brett, Brook, Lyric, and Kira with their solar-powered 1973 VW bus

SOLARROLLA, A COMPANY CONVERTING vehicles to fully electric, solar-powered living spaces, is run by Brett and Kira Belan.

In 2006, Brett and Kira met and began living off-grid in Northern California. Brett has a bachelor's degree in mechanical engineering and has been building cars since he was a teenager. He worked for Ford, then Jaguar in England, and later began setting up off-grid systems with solar, hydro, and wind power.

Brett and Kira loved the sustainability of creating their own power and decided they needed a vehicle that matched their ideals.

In 2008, they built a solar-powered golf cart. It performed so well that they began planning a full-size vehicle. Meanwhile, however, they converted a 1973 Harbilt English postal van, two more golf carts, and two Indian rickshaws. All of these were fully electric and solar-powered.

In 2012, they moved to Ashland, Oregon, and in 2015 began building their solar-powered 1973 VW bus, in which they have traveled with their family along the west coast.

In July, 2018, they formed Solarrolla Inc., and began building solar electric vehicles for others.

In 2018, they outfitted a 2011 Navistar eStar van with solar power and a larger battery pack for an Australian client, Joel Hayes. Joel formed Route Del Sol with a dream to drive a solar-powered vehicle on the Pan Am Highway all the way from Alaska to Argentina. (He has made it all the way to Baja at this point, purely on sun power.)

In 2019, they outfitted a 1971 VW bus for the singer/songwriter Redfoo; they consider this their most exceptional vehicle.

In that same year, they built a solar electric three-wheeled cargo bike and a mobile solar charging station on a trailer that can be used to charge an electric vehicle, as home backup for power outages, or other off-grid situations.

Recently, Brett and Kira moved from Oregon to a 12-acre piece of land in northern Wisconsin, which has a large shop with a car lift. They are currently working on two eStar vans; one for a client and one to use as a promotional and demonstration vehicle. They both will get up to 300 miles on a charge and will charge up to 100 miles a day from the sun. Also in process is another VW bus build and a 5 kW Solar pull-behind trailer to charge a Rivian Truck.

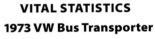

VITAL STATISTICS
1973 VW Bus Transporter

- 100-mile range
- Lithium ion battery pack
- 1200 watts of solar (4300W glass-framed panels)
- Up to 30 miles a day from the sun
- 6-hour charge time with Level 2 charging station
- High Performance Electric Vehicle Systems (HPEV) 500A, 144V AC electric motor
- Upper tent space for sleeping
- Ovente glass-top, electric, single-burner stove
- 23L Dometic AC/DC top-opening refrigerator
- Sink with 6-gallon storage tanks

Route del Sol eStar, Smith River, Oregon, 2019. (See next page.)

"What separates us from other car conversion companies is that all our vehicles have solar-powered roof arrays."

Solarrolla Philosophy

From an interview with Brett in December, 2021:

- What separates us from other car conversion companies is that all our vehicles have solar-powered roof arrays, making them off-grid, sustainable modes of travel in tiny homes.

- It might take 10 hours of charging to go 100 miles, so a van that you can live in while charging works well (as opposed to, say, a solar-powered electric bike). Take a nap! Make lunch!

- It's important to tilt the panels to track the sun as it moves across the sky.

- You can't really compare one of these with a gas-powered vehicle. Gasoline vehicles are more convenient, but look at the ecological devastation caused by just 100 years of burning fossil fuels.

- You will be slowing down. You won't need any gas. You won't have to pay rent. You'll be in tune with the sun … drive south?

- You don't go very far each day, but you interact with people and the landscape a lot more when you move more slowly.

- Think migration. Relax for a few days, harvest the sun's energy, then travel. (A solar-powered vehicle works great for Baja surfing trips.)

- Solar-powered vehicles are a lifestyle change. They are good for the heart, soul, and the planet.

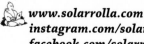
www.solarrolla.com
instagram.com/solarrolla
facebook.com/solarrolla

"Relax for a few days, harvest the sun's energy, then travel."

More…

Route del Sol eStar on Alaska Highway, 2018. Photos this page by Joel Hayes

VITAL STATISTICS
2011 Navistar eStar Van

- 200-mile range
- 2 lithium ion battery packs, primary LiFe pack is 80 kWh, secondary Íis 40 kWh of lithium nickel cobalt manganese (Li-NCM)
- 7900 watts of solar (24 330W flexible, aluminum-framed panels)
- Up to 100 miles a day from the sun
- 8-to-10-hour charge time with Level 2 charging station
- 70 kW, 102hp electric motor
- Ovente glass-top, electric, double-burner stove
- Top-opening refrigerator
- Sink with 16-gallon storage tanks
- Bathroom with shower and composting toilet

Baja California

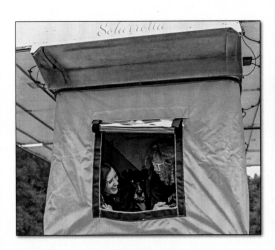

"Solar-powered vehicles are a lifestyle change."

"You will be slowing down. You won't need any gas. You won't have to pay rent."

VITAL STATISTICS
Redfoo 1971 VW Bus Transporter

- 100-mile range
- **Lithium Battery pack:** 7, Tesla Model S 5.3 kWh modules for a total of 37.5 kWh
- Almost 3,000 watts of solar (twelve 145W flexible, aluminum-framed panels)
- Up to 100 miles a day from the sun
- 4-hour charge time with Level 2 charging station, 2–3 with Tesla Destination charger
- NetGain Hyper9HV, 500A, 144V AC Electric Motor
- Upper tent space for sleeping and convertible couch/bed to sleep a total of 4
- Ovente glass-top, electric, single-burner stove
- 23L Dometic AC/DC top-opening refrigerator
- Sink with 6-gallon storage tanks

Just Camp!
Jon Burtt

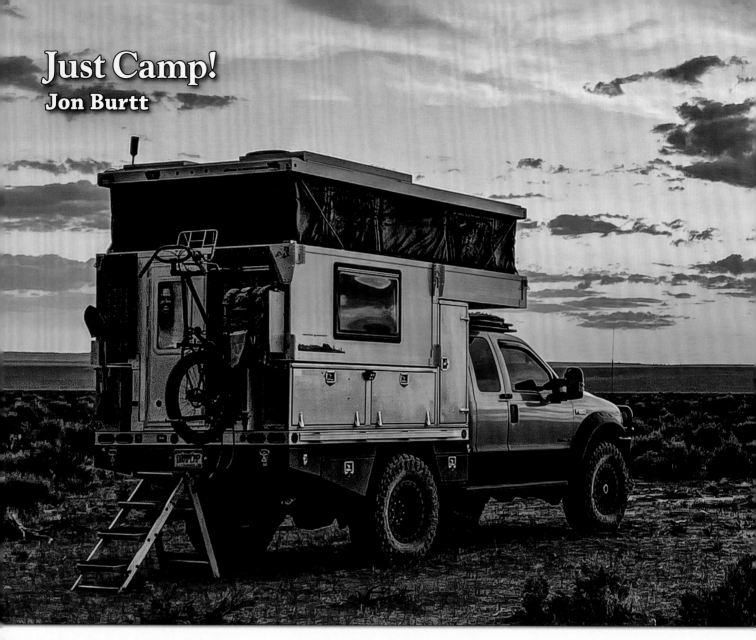

This is such a well worked-out rig! There's tons of useful information in the Vital Statistics here, informative for people outfitting their own off-road vehicles. (Recommended to us by Foster Huntington — see pp. 48–52.)

Here's Jon's account of building this vehicle and his life on the road: –LK

I'VE BEEN LIVING FOR TWO YEARS on the road with my dog Eocky.

I got into living in small spaces when I was a kid and I'd spend summers with my dad on his boat, camping, fishing, etc.

I grew up in the Midwest (Chicagoland area) and moved to Colorado after high school for college. I graduated with a degree in economics and shortly after,

worked at the Chicago Board of Trade in the commodity option pits. The crash hit and I opened up a detailing shop for exotics and modified vehicles.

Next I converted an Aairstream trailer into a gourmet kitchen and sold crèpes in Denver for about five years. During that time I started traveling in a Toyota Tacoma that I built up to tour around in. That vehicle got a lot of attention, as it was constantly evolving.

My next rig was the 2000 Ford F250 with the 7.3 liter engine (a great motor!) that you see here. As I continued to build up this Ford as an adventure vehicle, the more I loved it.

I found a used Four Wheel Hawk — an expandable flatbed camper unit — and

hit the road. At the time, nothing else was a big contender. I had to make a lot of changes to bring it up to par with today's technology, and to handle long trips and be stationary for a week or so. I made it work and lived in it for a solid year.

I was visiting a buddy's shop one day, and he had some new Overland Explorer campers from Canada. The moment I sat in one, I decided to sell what I had and get a new house for the back of the truck. Luckily, the way I'd put the flatbed, tunnel box and side storage boxes together, I was able to sit the new camper right down for a perfect fit.

While living in the road, I've launched a lifestyle brand about encouraging people to camp. It's called JustCamp.

If work was awful this week, just camp. Need to recharge? Just camp.

I think camping and this lifestyle can help people mentally and emotionally. It certainly has for me. It means you can get rid of all the stuff you don't need, but keep what's important. Plus you'll know who are your friends!

Just camp.

instagram.com/jonburtt
www.justcamp.us

Jon and his traveling buddy Eocky (who's part coyote) stopped by Shelter's production studio in 2021.

"I think camping and this lifestyle can help people mentally and emotionally."

More...

VITAL STATISTICS

- **Vehicle:** 2000 Ford F250 Super Duty
- **Motor:** International 7.3 L
- **2- or 4-wheel drive:** 4WD / automatic transmission
- **Suspension modification:** Swapped axles from a 2006 Ford F350 (front Dana 60 coil conversion and rear 10.5 Sterling) / 4.88 Nitro Gears / Auburn LSD rear / Old Man Emu 2.25" coils & shocks / custom Alcan rear leaf springs / Dynatrac Free Spin hub kit / Dynatrac ball joints / HD tie rod bar, drag link and trac bar
- **Cabin:** Scheelman Vario XLs in back / rear seat with two levels of storage for tools / dog platform / 50 qt. refrigerator mounted to rear seat
- **Rear :** Aluminum flatbed / custom aluminum full-width tunnel box, side-storage boxes & LineX'd under-tray boxes / OEV CampX composite slide-in camper mounted to flatbed
- **Fuel capacity:** About 800-mile fuel range from 55 gal. AeroTank replacement diesel tank mid ship / 5 gal. Nato spare diesel can on rear of camper
- **Sleeping:** Overland Explorer Camp X slide-in pop-top camper / queen-sized mattress on cab-over portion / dinette can sleep one adult or two kids comfortably
- **Water:** 20 gallons fresh water / stainless sink with faucet / quick-connect outdoor hot water shower near propane locker / 12V water pump
- **Cooking & refrigerator:** Dometic flush mounted two burner stove in countertop in the camper fed by two 11 lb. propane tanks outside in the propane locker / 73 qt. dual zone ARB Fridge in camper / 50 qt. ARB fridge for beverages in the cab of the truck / Partner Steel Khaya Stove one burner & Magma stainless grill in passenger-side aluminum storage box *aka* outdoor kitchen

- **Awnings:** Undecided, old camper had a Fiamma S45 awning which is likely what I'd add if ever decide it's needed again.

- **Camping chairs, tables:** Burl Big Leaf Maple dining table mounted inside the camper / 2 Snow Peak camp chairs / small Snow Peak folding table / exterior side storage doors act as tables whenever I need them as well.

- **Jumper cables, tow ropes, tire pumps, traction pads:** Jumper cables (stored under rear seat) / NOCO 4000A battery jump box (stored under passenger seat) / ARB Front Bull Bumper with ComeUp 12,500 lb. winch & synthetic line / Bubba rope & soft shackles / ARB tow strap & tree saver / 30 ft. of winch line extension / ARB dual air compressor / Maxtrax traction boards on Gamiviti roof rack using GPFactor mounts / shovel & axe on rear using Aluminess mount

- **Solar panels & power:** Truck Hood has 80W panel feeding engine batteries using Victron 75/15 MPPT solar charge controller / camper roof has two 195W panels / camper has two 100Ah Battle Born LiFePo4 batteries / Redarc Manager 30 / Xantrex 2000W inverter

- **Air heater:** Truma VarioHeat propane heater with thermostat

- **Ventilation fan:** Maxxair 10-speed automatic fan with remote

- **Shower, water heater:** Sagiva outside shower connection / Truma Aquago continuous propane hot water heater

- **Dometic dual-pane acrylic side window** with night shade and bug screen

- **Custom steel rear bumper** with hitch and recovery points

- **Roof rack:** Gamiviti roof rack

- **Snorkel:** TGM Airtec snorkel

- **Lighting:** Baja Designs throughout the entire rig and camper

- **Electronics:** Audio, Nav, Weboost and Ravelco systems

"As I continued to build up this Ford as an adventure vehicle, the more I loved it."

"Need to recharge? Just camp."

Homemade Pop-Top Camper

James Vadas

For several years, I made do with the small camper shell and cramped bed of my 2005 Toyota Tacoma while truck camping around the Rocky Mountains of Colorado. When my girlfriend, Alex, began joining me for my weekend adventures, I knew I needed to find a way to make the truck camping experience more comfortable and accommodating.

I found inspiration from a book about canoe building that described using epoxy to build waterproof and strong wooden canoes. I wondered if I could use the same process to build a wooden truck topper that would be lightweight, waterproof, and durable.

I created a rough design and began to assemble the tools and materials I would need for the wood and epoxy topper. I purchased ⅛″ plywood and light 2×4s from a local Home Depot, a three-gallon marine epoxy kit from Boat Builder Central and got to work. Over the course of three weeks, the topper took shape as I built the frame and sheathed it in thin plywood.

A feature I added to my topper was to extend the back end of the topper over the tailgate to allow easier access and provide more shelter at the back end of the truck. The topper was light and delicate, but as I applied several coats of marine epoxy, the topper hardened and stiffened.

"Total cost for materials: about $1,200, mostly from Lowe's and Home Depot."

I scavenged the windows and hardware from a damaged, old truck camper shell I bought on Craigslist. I sewed lightweight tent fabric to fit the pop-up opening and was given an old mattress foam pad to use as a bed in the topper's sleeping loft. Total cost for materials: about $1,200, mostly from Lowe's and Home Depot.

After four weeks, the topper was ready for the road. The benefits of the extra room and raised sleeping platform were immediately apparent. We no longer needed to shuffle our gear and belongings around when climbing into the bed to sleep at night. Now when we pull up to a trailhead or ski lot late at night, it's with the knowledge that we'll get the good night's sleep we want.

Rabbit Ears Pass, Colorado. It snowed 8″ that night and got down to 5 degrees Fahrenheit. We use a Mr. Buddy heater to warm the camper up at night before going to sleep and in the morning when waking up. It stays about 25 degrees warmer than outside. With the heater on low, it gets very toasty inside.

"...inspiration from canoe building, which uses epoxy to build waterproof, strong wooden canoes"

Overland Under Budget

Micah Weber

This is a thoughtfully designed, high-quality, homemade vehicle that Micah has tailored to his own individual needs. He's customized not only the camper shell, but a bunch of the truck parts — as you can see in the Vital Statistics on the following two pages. –LK

W HEN I FIRST GOT THIS TRUCK, IT WAS COMPLETELY STOCK, along with a camper shell. Although I made some small changes right away, like larger all-terrain tires and a little lift, the truck worked well for daily usage, weekend adventures, and the occasional multi-state road trip and off-road wonderings.

While it performed all the duties in its stock form, I knew there was room for improvement by tailoring it to fit my exact needs, and this is how this build came to be.

I learned that one of the most valuable aspects of designing something for your own use is that you no longer need to think about what will work for the masses; you can tailor its function to perfectly match your individual needs.

Inspired by the "ute trays" (customized flat beds) of Australia and utility/service vehicles here in the U.S., I decided to build my own flatbed and removable camper. I tried hard to ride the line of maximizing the size without going overboard and detracting from the off-road ability that's so useful with light and small trucks.

The new bed is both one foot wider and longer than the stock truck bed, giving me a huge surface for loading fun stuff like dirt bikes or less fun things like couches and fridges.

With the bed completely flat, I wanted to have storage for keeping useful tools and tie-downs that every truck should have. A pull-out rear tray and swing-out side Pelican storage cases allow access storage and extra fuel with or without the bed loaded or camper installed.

For the camper, the goal was to create a "mini hotel room" on the back of my truck and focus on a sleeping area, with cooking to be done outside. The increased bed size means we can sleep in the camper even with the lid closed.

The floor of the camper is nearly the exact dimensions of a queen-size mattress and with the top raised up and upper sleeping platform pulled out, the whole family can comfortably sleep with almost zero setup time.

Overall, I'm extremely happy with the results. The feeling you get from building to your specific needs and getting to use your creation as envisioned is something you can't buy.

youtube.com/overlandunderbudget
instagram.com/overlandunderbudget
www.overlandunderbudget.com

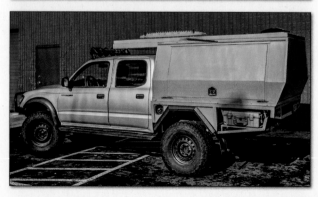

"I decided to build my own flatbed and removable camper."

More…

VITAL STATISTICS

- 2001 Toyota Tacoma SR5 TRD
- **Purchase price:** $7,500 in 2019
- **Mileage:** 208,000, now 255,000
- Custom flatbed and removable camper
- **Driveline and suspension:**
  - **Gears:** 4:88 Nitro gears
  - Rear factory e-locker
  - Front ARB air locker
  - **Rear suspension:** Custom home-made leaf pack, plus Firestone Ride-Rite air bags on Daystar cradles
  - **Front suspension:** 12-year-old Kings 2.5 (that desperately need rebuilding), SPC upper control arms, new factory ball joints
- **Wheels:** Toyota "spare tire" steel wheels, 16×7 with 1.2" Hub Centric spacers
- **Tires:** BF Goodrich all-terrain 285/75 R16 BFG A KO2
- **Armor:** Front bumper: Coastal off-road closed-top winch bumper
- **Winch:** Warn VR-EVO 10S winch
- **IFS and belly skid:** Homemade
- **Rock sliders:** Homemade
- **Roof light bar:** Homemade, with Amazon lights
- **Interior upgrades:** Custom dash with 10-inch touch screen and Apple car play; powered leather seats from a 2006 Mercedes ML; removable fridge platform behind the driver seat

"I knew there was room for improvement by tailoring it to fit my exact needs."

"The whole family can comfortably sleep with almost zero setup time."

total length
10 ft.

7.5 ft.
height open

6.5 ft.
camper floor length

4×4 Cabin

Kevin Smith

"Why not compile all my favorite ideas and build a dream camper?"

THOUGH I DIDN'T REALIZE IT AT THE time, the groundwork for building this camper began over 20 years ago when I was learning how to weld in high school metal shop and dreaming of living in the mountains.

My first camper was a fiberglass shell on a 4×4 Nissan truck with a simple DIY interior. This rig opened up a whole new world to me: I could go anywhere, yet be at home while snowboarding, surfing, cycling, hiking, kayaking, and exploring the outdoors. I eventually upgraded to a pop-up truck camper, lived in it full-time for a few years, and learned how camper design can have a big impact on long-term comfort.

The thought eventually dawned on me, "Why not combine all my favorite ideas and build a dream camper?"

There was really nothing available to buy that had everything I was looking for. I began planning with hand drawings and compiling a list of "must have" features. Once I got a final vision, I'd draw a picture and hang it on the wall until the camper was completed.

I built the camper in my backyard over two years using a portable MIG welder, power hand tools, a small sheet metal brake, and a sewing machine.

I ignored deadlines, and kept the focus on quality and simplicity. Taking short trips with the camper in an unfinished state helped the design evolve. I learned that design ideas often come at their own pace.

I aimed for the camper to be a space that would feel open and enjoyable on a stormy day. I wanted to drink coffee in the morning surrounded by windows with outdoor views.

The interior is seven feet tall to fit my 6'5" height and allow surfboards to be hung from the ceiling. The camper is large enough for me to feel content while on the road for long travels but small enough to go most places.

A long side compartment is specifically designed to house a quiver of snowboards, and a flip-down door provides a work bench for waxing. Additional outside storage carries gear for multiple sports and hobbies.

Building a camper from the ground up pushed my design and fabrication skills to a new level. In the future, I plan to explore more of North America while feeling at home on the road.

VITAL STATISTICS

- **Truck:** 2018 Ram 3500 4×4 chassis cab 84″, dual-axle
- **Engine:** Cummins 6.7 diesel
- **Transmission:** 6-speed manual
- **Camper Construction:**
  - **Framing, walls and ceiling:** Welded steel, 16-gauge square and rectangular tubing
  - **Framing, floor frame:** ⅛″ thick square tubing
  - **Fastening:** Attached to truck frame with grade 8 bolts
  - **Heating:** Cubic Mini Cub woodstove and Espar Airtronic D2 diesel-powered forced-air heater
- **Water System:** 26 gal. fresh water tank that supplies: foot pump to sink faucet (DIY soldered copper), gravity-feed spigot in doorway, pump-to-trigger-handle shower sprayer on hose in doorway. Greywater from sink feeds into portable 5 gal. jug in an exterior compartment, allowing for easy greywater disposal.
- **Electrical:**
  - Two 100Ah Battleborn lithium batteries
  - DC-to-DC charger (charges battery as engine runs)
  - 200W solar panels to be added to roof in future
  - 2000W inverter to be added in future
- **Cooking:** Propane 3-burner stove with oven
- **Refrigerator:** High-efficiency 12V ARB 50-qt. fridge/freezer
- **Bathroom:** Self-contained cassette Thetford Porta Potti is stored under a flip-up couch seat.

Other features:
- Cabover bed extends over kitchen to become 5′ wide, 7'2″ long.
- Pull-out fridge is on 500 lb. drawer slides, and doubles as a step for entering the bed.
- Curtains made from Mexican blankets purchased in Baja. I sewed in "blackout" fabric backing so they block all light.
- Cushions made using a dense upholstery foam to allow for sitting cross-legged on couches.
- Table is removable and has three configurations:
  - Attached to wall
  - Rotated 180 degrees so couch can be transformed into U-shaped booth
  - Lowered to create bed
- Diesel heater is located near lithium batteries and toilet to allow for passive warming in cold climates.
- Walls are 2″ thick and insulated with R-Max rigid foam in stud cavities (R-13 insulation value).
- All plumbing is routed through the interior to prevent freezing.
- Top-loading storage was utilized where possible so it's impossible for anything to fall out on bumpy roads.
- All drawers have automatic spring-loaded latches, to prevent unintended opening.
- Aluminum "L-Track" mounted on inside of ceiling to allow for movable attachment points. Various uses include: attachment of gear nets for additional storage, drying lines for wet clothes, gymnastics rings and/or yoga hammock, as well as for hanging surfboards.

---

 instagram.com/snowsurfadventurerig

"I ignored deadlines, and kept
the focus on quality and simplicity."

More...

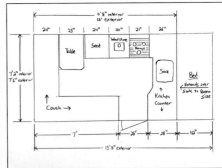

"Building a camper from the ground up pushed my design and fabrication skills to a new level."

Minaret Vista, Mammoth Lakes, California

Stormy morning, Schweitzer Mountain, Idaho

Surfing at Tres Alejandros, near Punta Santa Rosalilita (Seven Sisters), Baja California

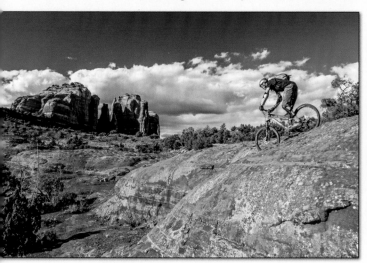

Biking in Sedona, Arizona

Kayaking, East Fork, Kaweah River, Tulare County, California

"I could go anywhere, yet be at home while snowboarding, surfing, cycling, hiking, kayaking, and exploring the outdoors."

Snowboarding, Schweitzer Mountain, Idaho

Surfer's $500 Camper Shell

Gabriel Abrego

Photos by Nick Radford

I'VE RECENTLY HIT THE STAGE IN LIFE where responsibilities are at an all-time high. Getting married, raising kids, running a business, doing house chores, paying bills — the list goes on.

I love to surf, but my windows for surfing have become few and far between. These windows are precious, so I need to be very selective, always paying attention so that when the surf is up, I'm ready to go.

I decided that what I needed was a camper shell on my existing 2013 Toyota Tacoma work truck — to house all my surf gear, camping supplies, and provide a place to sleep (whether that's in a campground, dirt road, or parking lot).

I needed the build to be low-budget. It also would have to be a part-time side project as it couldn't interfere with any of my work in in our full-time furniture shop.

I nickel-and-dimed my time on the camper shell for about a year. I used as many shop remnant materials as I could, and anything I bought was easily available from the local hardware store.

I spent around $500 in total, $200 of which was a failed attempt at using epoxy and fiberglass over the hollow "basket weave" roof. The main structure is made of 2×3 Douglas fir, with an upper level that cantilevers over the cab of the truck — creating an 8′ × 3½′ sleeping platform. The platform has a trap door on hinges, which allows access from underneath and can be closed to create the sleeping space.

There are two holes in the platform, which allow soft racks to be strapped down so longer surfboards can be secured while driving. The "basket weave" roof is scrap Baltic ply strips interwoven and skinned with a ballistic nylon that is sealed with a two-part urethane — essentially the same application as a modern skin-on-frame canoe.

Insulated grocery bags were used as insulation and the interior of the

"I love to surf, but my windows for surfing have become few and far between."

shell is finished with scrap cedar strips. Front and back windows open to create a breezeway and a nice view for the morning surf check.

The lower area in the bed of the truck had to be simple so I could still use the truck for loading lumber. A simple shelf of Baltic ply is mounted to the ceiling, utilizing eye hooks with bungees to secure camping and surf gear.

The back hatch is fully functioning, with two hinges, actuators, and locking hardware. The whole hatch is completely removable with an Allen key.

Curtains were made from scrap cotton fabric sewn by my wife and hung by bungee cords that runs through the sewn loops, keeping them taut.

I'm sure there will be new ideas for improvements and changes to be made based on how everything works on the road. In the meantime, the camper shell helps solve a problem and has brought some ideas to life. Now I wait for the next window....

"I needed the build to be low-budget.... I spent around $500 in total."

"The 'basket weave' roof is scrap Baltic plywood strips interwoven and skinned with a ballistic nylon that is sealed with a two-part urethane."

 instagram.com/abregocaravans, instagram.com/abregodesign
Blog: *abregodesign.com, abregocaravans.com*

The Vardo Camper
Addison Carter

"It has a full-size bed and comfortable seating for more than two."

BUILT ON A '98 V6 TOYOTA TACOMA, THE camper is framed with Douglas fir 2×2s and 2×4s and insulated with 1½˝ rigid foam. It's sheathed with ¼˝ and ⅜˝ plywood with a redwood bender-board ceiling on top of custom Douglas fir glue-laminated arches and then sided with ⅜˝ clear cedar T&G.

It is meticulously glued, screwed, caulked, sanded, oiled, and varnished. The roof is a temporary pond liner but it will eventually be copper.

It has a total of eight hidden tie-down points, four of which are turnbuckles that go through the truck bed to the frame, and the other four are ratchet straps to the bed's tie-down points. It has four detachable Rieco-Titan hydraulic legs that operate manually or with a drill.

The interior is paneled with cedar bender-boards and built out with lightweight cedar-framed cabinets and shelving. It has a full-size bed and comfortable seating for more than two.

It has a full kitchen with a three-burner propane stove/oven with a hood vent, running water, 12V fridge/freezer, and a Dickinson marine propane heater. It holds 21 gallons of water and 11 pounds of propane.

Powered by a 12-volt lithium ion 170Ah Renogy battery with two 170-watt, flexible Renogy solar panels. The camper battery

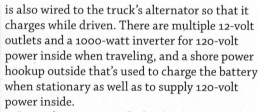

is also wired to the truck's alternator so that it charges while driven. There are multiple 12-volt outlets and a 1000-watt inverter for 120-volt power inside when traveling, and a shore power hookup outside that's used to charge the battery when stationary as well as to supply 120-volt power inside.

It weighs 1,700 pounds dry (maximum payload of a stock Tacoma) and was designed so I could eventually transplant it onto a slightly larger truck with a custom flatbed for extra storage as well as water and propane.

With the help of many good friends, this camper was built a few feet from my bed in the middle of my house (which is a garage that I renovated to be a living space/workshop). Griffin Johnston and Austin Leddusire are a couple of those good friends. Griffin made sure I didn't breathe in too much sawdust all by myself, and Austin gave life to the camper with electricity. We spent hundreds of hours working on it and pulled a lot of all-nighters: building until the sun came up, listening to Peter Cat Recording Co., and drinking really good coffee. It was crazy, the most fun I've ever had, and I can't wait to do it again.

 *www.vardocampers.com*

"With the help of many good friends, this camper was built a few feet from my bed...."

The $300 Camper Shell
Noah Gavrich

More...

This is one of my favorite designs in the book: the simplicity of necessity; the flip side of the tricked-out Sprinter van.

The curved roof feels spacious (like gypsy wagons), the corrugated metal is strong and cheap, and the bed/table arrangement works well.

I'll bet this is going to inspire some similar rigs. —LK

I FIRST BECAME INTERESTED IN sustainable living in high school, while taking an environmental studies course. For my final project, I made a rough design for a completely off-grid home. After seeing how much work I put into the project, my teacher gave me her copy of *Home Work*. My mind was properly blown, and for the rest of high school, and my successive time in art school, I had a fantasy of designing my own camper.

Growing up in San Francisco, I was familiar with companies doing expensive retrofitting, charging $20,000–$50,000 to deck out an already expensive Sprinter van.

I figured I could design and build something original that would fit my needs for only a few hundred bucks, using a lot of recycled materials. So, finding myself with some free time, I decided to make something that could fit the bed of my truck.

I built and designed the camper as I went, with help from my neighbors John and Dorothy, over the course of a few months. It was completed for a total cost of around $300, and half of the materials were found or recycled.

"The camper itself can be lifted into place by one person."

I wanted the build to be as light and drag-resistant as possible, so the sides are made of plywood, a tin roof mounted to arches cut from a three-quarter sheet of plywood and doubled up, and a slanted plexiglass front that acts as a skylight.

The side lifts up so I can wake up with a view, but the design component of which I am most proud is the bed platform — the first of its kind. The centerpiece of the bed can be placed on the side shelf to act as a table inside the camper, or all three pieces can be removed and assembled into a standing table outside.

The bed platform and shelves are freestanding and can be assembled in a few minutes, and the camper itself can be lifted into place by one person with some ratchet straps on high rafters.

The interior becomes a cozy bed when the seat cushion squares are assembled to fill the space and covered with a quilt —both of which were designed by my girlfriend, Juliet. (It's incredibly comfy, we swear!)

We have a foldup solar panel and compact 500-watt all-in-one battery, charger, and inverter that we use to power our ceiling lights and charge our laptops so we can work or watch a movie while on a trip.

VITAL STATISTICS
- **Car:** 2001 Toyota Tacoma
- **Roofing:** Galvanized sheets, attached with screws with rubber washers
- **Miles:** 170,000
- **Mileage:** 22.5 mpg., loaded down
- **Battery:** 500W Jackery
- 100 foldable Rockpals solar panel

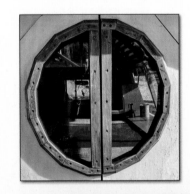

Photos of Noah and Juliet by Gina Randazzo

"It was completed for a total cost of around $300,
and half of the materials were found or recycled."

More...

"The sides are made of plywood, a tin roof mounted to arches cut from a three-quarter sheet of plywood."

*"It's incredibly comfy,
we swear!"*

Lightweight Camper Shell
Triston Wu

"Strong winds swept across the Great Salt Lake and rocked the truck, but she held fast in the night."

I BEGAN CONSTRUCTION OF THE CAMPER in March of 2021 in the driveway of my girlfriend's house. A design had been bouncing around in my head for quite some time. First, I constructed a simple wooden structure using stock lumber and scrap wood. I laminated strips of redwood bender board typically used for gardening to achieve the arched ceiling.

Next, I skinned the structure in two-inch EPS home insulation using spray insulation as glue. I then fiberglassed with epoxy and finished with a gel coat made for boats.

With the shell done, I started the interior by laying ¼-inch plywood down as a floor. I built a bed using Ikea slats and 2×2 Douglas fir. Half the bed slides out and rests on the shelf, allowing it to double as a bench and bed. The shelf features a plywood drawer with aluminum angle iron as drawer slides. The interior was designed to use a minimal amount of material and save weight.

The main design challenge was to keep the camper lightweight to reduce adverse effects on the handling of the truck. I had to make a 4-cylinder, 2002 Tacoma with stock suspension work. Although underpowered, the truck was in superb condition with only 61,000 miles.

This base model Tacoma features a luxurious analog interior with manual windows, cloth bench seat, three cup holders, working A/C, and a simple three-gauge dash. The only maintenance needed was a spark plug change and headlight restoration. The only way I could measure the camper shell was to pick it up and step on a scale, then subtract my weight. The end weight was roughly 300 pounds!

We had not yet planned a route, accommodations, and all the other small things to plan when embarking on a big trip. All we knew for certain was that we were going to drive across the United States. We left just as a heat wave hit the West Coast. Las Vegas greeted us with a high of 115 and we couldn't have been more grateful for working A/C.

A sudden thunderstorm was the first true waterproofing test for the camper. The door leaked a bit, so I added a lip to the roof. It helped divert water and pushed turbulence farther away from the back of the truck on the highway.

Next stop was Spiral Jetty, near Salt Lake City, Utah. We arrived in the dark, on a dirt road that cut through grass fields and hills. Strong winds swept across the Great Salt Lake and rocked the truck, but she held fast in the night.

VITAL STATISTICS

- **Vehicle:** 2002 Toyota Tacoma 2×4, 4-cylinder
- **Odometer:** 69,900
- **Mileage:** Avg. 23 highway, 19 city
- **Camper materials:** Pine, redwood, salvaged wood, 2" EPS foam insulation from Home Depot, fiberglass, boat gel coat
- **Steel roof rack**
- **Interior lights:** rechargeable LED puck lights, rechargeable Coleman lantern
- **Refrigerator:** Yeti Hopper flip cooler
- **Stoves:** Coleman single-burner butane stove, MSR Pocket Rocket
- **Water:** 5 gal. collapsible tank

"Half the bed slides out and rests on the shelf, allowing it to double as a bench and bed."

"The end weight was roughly 300 pounds!"

Surfing at Swamis, Encinitas, California

The Birdhouse
Home-Built Truck Camper
Brandon Doherty & Elizabeth Heym

"After the long building process, we are finally living full-time in this cabin on wheels."

THE BIRDHOUSE IS A FULLY CUSTOM-built truck camper designed to fit the back of a Ford F250 flatbed. It's planned as a rugged yet spacious permanent home for two climbers on the move. Being climbers, we knew a lot about the concept of "vanlife." However, we wanted a more cost-effective and warm environment compared to today's typical Sprinter van conversion.

With Brandon's professional design background and master's degree in architecture, we felt the construction of a completely custom truck camper was an exciting challenge.

The camper is framed like a traditional house, with 2×4 studs, and the pine tongue-and-groove exterior sheathing is assembled so it's waterproof.

Due to weight concerns, the structure has let-in braces and Simpson anchors in place of traditional plywood sheathing.

The windows are custom built from cherry lumber offcuts from the local lumberyard. There are three round portholes, and two operable awning windows, in addition to the skylight. Each window is glazed with flexible polycarbonate.

The inside walls are lined with ¼-inch cedar closet lining, which is then trimmed out with small offcuts from the process of building the windows.

The interior is organized with a long kitchen counter on one side and a bench with storage space underneath opposite. On the kitchen side we have our used RV stove, home-built sink, Dometic refrigerator, and Goal Zero battery (powered by three Renogy solar panels). Also in the camper is a Nature's Head composting toilet.

Opposite the kitchen, the bench folds up where we store dry food and clothing. All of the climbing and outdoor gear is stored in the cab of the truck to keep the camper clean. At the end of the couch is a small wood burning stove.

The full build process from research to move-in took just over a year, working late nights and weekends. After the long building process, we are finally living full-time in this cabin on wheels.

VITAL STATISTICS

- **Truck:** Used 2001 Ford F250 Diesel with 7.3L engine, converted to a custom flatbed and 4-wheel drive by previous owner. Leaf springs upgraded to the F350 model.

- **General Camper:** Framed from scratch, essentially the same as a tiny house. We built the windows from cherry lumber short cuts we picked up at the local lumberyard. We found the door in an alley by our apartment. The camper is built as a removable unit so we can change trucks if necessary. We also built a pass-through to allow us to move between the cab and the camper without going outside.

- **Exterior siding:** Tongue-and-groove pine

- **Insulation:** Havelock Wool batts

- **Roof:** Plywood with a liquid rubber coating painted on

- **Appliances:** Used RV stove and Dometic 95L refrigerator (bought at REI garage sale)

- **Power station:** Goal Zero Yeti 1500x

- **Solar charging:** 3 Renogy 100W solar panels

- **Woodstove:** Cubic mini woodstove, with Dickinson Marine stainless steel flue pipe

- **Kitchen sink:** Custom copper sink and brass faucet

- **Ventilation:** Maxxair roof vent

> "We wanted a more cost-effective and warm environment compared to today's typical Sprinter van conversion."

Bridge in background is the New River Gorge Bridge on US Route 19, just outside Fayetteville, North Carolina

Lotus Pod

Stevie Hudson and Margarita Prokofyeva

> *"After a couple of weeks of tireless work, we were ready to hit the road!"*

I HAD BEEN DREAMING OF BUILDING A house truck ever since I saw how epic they could be in Lloyd's book *Tiny Homes on the Move*. I'd seen plenty of vans, had already built, traveled, and lived in a tiny house on wheels, and was awe inspired by the sailboats, but the trucks were what really stuck with me.

For a while I thought it would be a big 1950s International truck or something where I'd rip the bed off as a starting point (which I still want to do), but more than anything, I just wanted to build a personal travel rig as soon as possible.

So in the middle of building our second tiny house we decided to stop everything and work with what we had to bring the first iteration of the Wonder Wagon tiny house on wheels to life: The Lotus Pod. *(See pp. 222–225.)*

This rig was designed to be extremely simple so that we could use it for extended road trips rather than full-time living, while still being fully usable as my work truck and daily driver.

We built a simple platform with two 8-foot drawers underneath, which, along with the cantilever, provided ample storage for everything two people would need.

The cedar shakes, local poplar, and heart pine for the interior siding, sheep's wool insulation, handmade windows, and silk-upholstered headboard were all leftovers from the Wonder Wagon tiny house build. After a couple of weeks of tireless work, we were ready to hit the road!

We traveled from Virginia to Vermont, across upstate New York, through the Midwest, all around Colorado and then back to finish the Wonder Wagon. On our trip we visited family and friends, jumped in waterfalls, backpacked 14ers, *(mountains 14,000 feet or higher)*, went white-water rafting, sledded on sand dunes, skinny-dipped in cold mountain streams, fed our souls in the forests, mountain biked in the Rockies, stayed up stargazing and dreaming in the high desert, meditated with stunning views, and much more.

I wouldn't trade these experiences on the road for anything and if I had one thing to say to anyone reading it would be this —don't let fear and doubt get in the way of manifesting and realizing your desires and dreams. You are a part of source energy, and because of that, you can do anything!

instagram.com/WonderRigs
www.WonderRigs.com

> *"I just wanted to build a personal travel rig as soon as possible."*

"I wouldn't trade these experiences on the road for anything."

VITAL STATISTICS

- 2002 Chevy Silverado 1500 V6 120,000 mi.
- Coleman camp stove
- Whynter LLC refrigerator/freezer
- Havelock wool insulation
- Goal Zero battery and solar panel

Stealth Camper Shell

Johnny Vang

Early one spring evening I was on my way home from Mendocino County and stopped to get dinner at a Vietnamese restaurant near Santa Rosa. On the way back to my car, I noticed this unusual rig, looking a bit like a homemade armored car.

Since I'd been working on this book (and thinking a lot about nomadic living), I wondered if this could be a camper unit. There were no windows, but I noticed what looked like a vent above the rear door. Then, in looking into the cab, I saw a curtain behind the seat, which looked like it could be a passageway from the truck into the camper shell.

I knocked on the side and sure enough, there was an inhabitant: Johnny Vang. Johnny said he and three friends had been paying $800 each per month to rent a house and that's what motivated him to go nomadic.

He has a production job, working the night shift and sleeping during the day. He said that as far as getting hassled for living in a truck, security is much more lax during daytime hours.

He bought the truck, used, which has an LM7 5.3-liter, 8-cylinder Vortec engine, for $3,200. "I love this motor," he says, which now has 298,000 miles on it and gets 15 miles per gallon at 70 miles per hour.

In design, he followed the lines of the cab for aerodynamics. He said not having a skylight minimized chances of a break-in. He spent about $2,000 on materials for the shell.

I was surprised by the efficient yet homey atmosphere of the interior, compared to the stern exterior. Johnny doesn't have any design credentials, but this is a well thought-out, practical design.

Johnny is Hmong; he and his parents immigrated to this country from Laos in the 1980s, settling in Central California. He is the first generation born in California.

*He's considering building more of these and can be contacted at **johnnyturbogt@gmail.com**.*

–LK

> **"In design, he followed the lines of the cab for aerodynamics."**

VITAL STATISTICS

- **Vehicle:** 2004 Chevy Silverado 1500 RWD
- **Camper shell:** Frame is 1.5″ × 1.5″ 0.065-thick square tubing. Panels are 5052 aluminum at 0.040 thickness. I used ³⁄₁₆″ aluminum rivets with various grip sizes, according to the thickness of materials being held together.
- **Insulation:** R-5 1.5″ polystyrene foam board insulation from Lowe's
- **Pass-through:** Truck has a pass-through into cab and the truck cab to bed is mated/sealed using an accordion boot.
- **Stove:** Basic Coleman portable stove
- **Refrigeration:** Engel 40 qt. cooler
- **Water:** 14 gal. tank with Seaflo water pump
- **Greywater:** 7 gal. greywater tank with Harbor Freight electric water pump to pump out water
- **Toilet:** Custom-made compost toilet using Aspen wood chips
- **Cooling:** Push-and-pull fans from Amazon
- **Batteries:** Four 35Ah Deep Cycle AGM batteries from Harbor Freight; Perko battery switch to keep batteries charged when driving or idling
- **Upgrades:** The only thing I'm going to redo with this setup is the toilet, which I'll put in a pull-out drawer. I'll add a 20 gal. fresh water tank where the spare tire mounts under the truck.
- **Advice to the DIY-inclined:** Plan very carefully. Build, then rebuild. It's all part of the vanlife game. What works for you now might not work later on. You'll find innovative changes as time passes to make your life on wheels more comfortable. Change is inevitable when building a home on wheels.
- Last but not least, you're not homeless — just houseless.

> **"Change is inevitable when building a home on wheels."**

³⁄₁₆" aluminum pop rivets attach
metal panels to frame.

"'I love this motor,' he says, which now has 298,000 miles
on it and gets 15 miles per gallon at 70 miles per hour."

Accordion boot
from cab to
truck bed

Curtain covering opening
to bed behind seat

More...

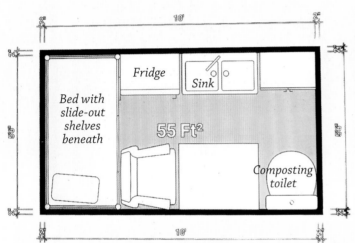

Johnny's bed is sideways, behind driver's seat, reachable through side door (or through driver's seat). Would work less well for tall people.

Two levels of storage under bed — from driver's side

Under-bed storage from passenger side

10'

Fridge

Sink

Bed with slide-out shelves beneath

55 Ft²

Composting toilet

10'

Deep cell batteries under bed

"He spent about $2,000 on materials for the shell."

> "Plan very carefully. Build, then rebuild.
> It's all part of the vanlife game."

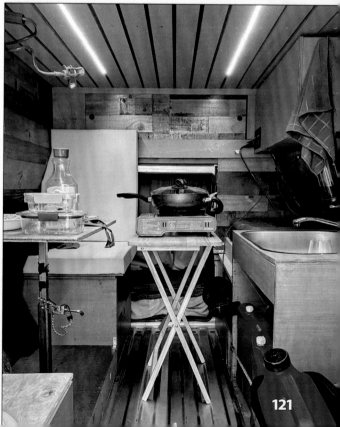

121

The Beehive
Chris Rodiger

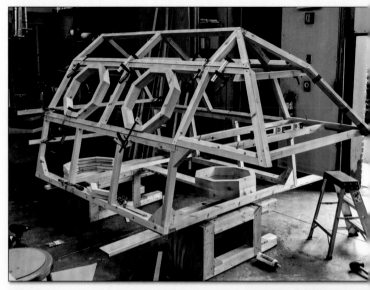

AROUND THE START OF THE COVID-19 PANDEMIC, I WAS diagnosed with metastatic cancer. During the many months of treatments, I turned to painting to escape the pain my body was going through.

As I completed my recovery, my creative practice became a strong source of identity, therapy, and meaning.

I began dreaming of a space that would allow me to break free from the studio and dive into the landscapes I was painting. I wanted to recapture that childlike state of wonder that makes self-expression so powerful.

Enter: The Beehive.

The concept was inspired by the work of artists like Jay Nelson *(see pp. 132–135)* and Foster Huntington *(see pp. 48–51)*, who have motivated me to live by my own design.

It all started with a few ridiculous drawings and a dream.

During my third year at Colby College (in Waterville, Maine), I created an independent study course, submitted a proposal, and received a grant to construct a livable space on my truck bed. I bought the smallest truck I could find with low mileage, and a six-foot bed. After 500 hours of work, challenging geometry problems, and backbreaking nights sleeping on the studio table hidden behind cabinets, the Beehive became my home.

The whole structure is entirely handbuilt and designed using Maine white cedar. The exterior is sealed with six coats of spar urethane.

The doors and interior furnishings are made from marine and birch plywood. The four octagonal porthole windows open up in true land yacht fashion.

Three main sections are held together via carriage bolts, which can be disassembled and stored away when not in use. Because it is built out of cedar, the Beehive weighs less than 500 pounds.

The summer of 2021, I lived and worked out of the Beehive selling paintings and getting commissions while traveling up and down the Maine coast. My dream is to eventually teach and work full-time as a painter.

"My dream is to eventually teach and work full-time as a painter."

122

> *"The concept was inspired by the work of artists like Jay Nelson and Foster Huntington, who have motivated me to live by my own design."*

> *"The whole structure is entirely handbuilt and designed using Maine white cedar."*

VITAL STATISTICS

- **Vehicle:** 2011 Ford Ranger, 4 cylinder, 5-speed manual transmission, great fuel economy, tiny footprint, fun to drive, only 55,000 mi. on it
- **Water:** A good ol' gallon jug
- **Heating:** A sleeping bag
- **Appliances:** Coleman butane stove
- **Bed:** 6´ bench bed with storage for painting supplies underneath. Plywood insert allows room for two.

Note: As of late 2021, Chris has been cancer-free for a year and a half.
                                                                          —LK

www.chrisrodigerart.com
instagram.com/chrisrodigerart
facebook.com/chrisrodigerart

Aerodynamic Toyota Camper Shell

Joel Wolpert

"The key lesson I learned while building it was to accept every mistake that was not structural."

I BUILT IT IN 2015 AND RENOVATED IT in 2018. It sits at the intersection between the paralyzing perfectionism of my youth and my current joy at building curious crafts.

The idea was to build an aerodynamic camper for a Toyota Tacoma. I had already built a wood-strip kayak and bathtub before I saw Jay Nelson's famous Honda Civic camper. *(See Jay's creations on pp. 132–135, and also in Tiny Homes on the Move.)* The stage was set for a massive extrapolation.

After a few months of tinkering and procrastinating on the framework, I stripped out the camper in a frenzy of long nights. It took eight days to lay all the strips, a day and a half to sand it; one day was spent glassing the outside, and three days went into building the back bottom extension. The day I attached the door, it hit the highway.

The key lesson I learned while building it was to accept every mistake that was not structural…and maybe a few that were.

The thing I love most about it is that it accidentally became the most successful public art project I have ever been involved with. It simply exists in the world and functions to showcase the hilarious possibilities.

I meet people whom I would never meet otherwise. Nearly everyone wants to make sense of it as some sort of animalistic form, to figure out what it's supposed to be.

In reality, it is much less imaginative: it is supposed to be aerodynamic. And it is. It can get up to 20 miles per gallon.

www.thewolpertinger.com
instagram.com/the.wolpertinger

"I meet people whom I would never meet otherwise."

VITAL STATISTICS

- **Vehicle:** 2003 Toyota Tacoma
- **Materials:** ⅛"-thick White Pine strips from Helvetian Timber Works here in West Virginia; plywood; 6 oz. fiberglass (3 layers outside / 1 layer inside) and West System marine-grade epoxy
- Polka dots (for speed)
- Metal flake (for allure)

"It accidentally became the most successful public art project I have ever been involved with."

"It is supposed to be aerodynamic. And it is.
It can get up to 20 miles per gallon."

Pickup Truck Sauna

Bennett Gates

"I wanted to make a sauna that I could tow to the ski resorts."

I WAS STARTING MY FINAL YEAR OF UNIVERSITY WHEN I decided I wanted to make a sauna that I could tow to the ski resorts near Kelowna, British Columbia. Having grown up in California, I never got used to the colder temperatures up here, and a sauna would hopefully be a game changer.

I had made a few surfing trips out to Vancouver Island and wanted this project to double as something that would make it easier to stay warmer before and after surf sessions.

In September 2019, I started in the basement of the house I had lived in for the previous three years with my college roommates. The main frames and back portion with the door were assembled in the basement over most of the winter.

I was extremely lucky to have roommates that put up with copious amounts of sawdust and noise. My roommate Bill actually lived in the basement and had only a curtain separating him from my work area. His belongings were constantly covered in a layer of dust, and without his carefree attitude, the project wouldn't have been possible.

Once the weather started heating up, the assembly was finished outside. Once again, I called on my roommates to help; we maneuvered each pre-assembled large frame up a narrow and steep stairway to the outside. A few holes in the drywall later and it was now time to finish assembling it in the backyard.

The project was way behind schedule and the end goal for it was starting to morph. I had grown impatient and jumped on the opportunity to purchase a cedar barrel sauna from Craigslist.

"This meant there was only one other place to put the homemade sauna—my pickup. I figured it would now be a camper."

After fixing a few things, it was working flawlessly and was now on the flat deck trailer originally meant for the homemade sauna. This meant there was only one other place to put the homemade sauna—my pickup.

I figured it would now be a camper. I added a bed that doubled as a table, some basic shelves for storage, a solar panel with inverter and lights, and a bamboo cross-country ski pole for hanging clothes. The final challenge was raising the camper up to a height of 35 inches so it could slide onto the truck bed.

With the help of three farm jacks, six dining room chairs, lots of wood offcuts, and a strong strapping fellow named Paul, it just barely fit onto the truck.

The truck and camper currently are parked in Victoria, BC, and the camper has been in constant use across the province ever since it was mounted on the truck. I plan to build more campers, saunas, and cabins.

 instagram.com/benitgates

VITAL STATISTICS

Truck:
- **Model:** 2005 Ford F250
- **Transmission:** ZF 6-speed manual, 4×4
- **Engine:** 5.4L

Camper:
- **Dimensions:** 8′ long × 6′ wide at widest point
- **Heat:** Custom backyard-welded stove that is completely air-sealed on the inside. Wood is loaded from outside to avoid danger of carbon monoxide or oxygen depletion.
- Acrylic front window
- **Siding:** Red cedar
- Sleeps two while having lots of storage for gear
- Surfboard side rack
- Teardrop shape allows for convenient storage in truck bed sides.
- **Solar panel:** 100W with lithium ion phosphate 170Ah battery from old communication tower
- **Weight:** Around 1,000 lbs.

"*The truck and camper currently are parked in Victoria, BC, and the camper has been in constant use…ever since it was mounted on the truck.*"

Flutter By Pizza Pie

Mark Ennis

Photos by Daniel Burgess

Hey Lloyd,
I'm a huge fan of your work and it's been super inspirational to me on my journey. So it was sweet when some of my friends tagged me in your post seeking contributions from folks who make sweet rigs under $100,000—because that's me!

Flutter By Pizza Pie started with a pizza oven made with a Coleman grill lid found on the side of Highway 1 six years ago, and I have dedicated myself to building out this dream ever since: a wood-burning pizza truck that feeds people on the Olympic Peninsula in Washington.

It's a truck, it's a kitchen, it's a dream, it's a home, it's science fiction—I guess most of all, it's a living commitment to building a more harmonious world. A world that centers the imagination, art, and sourcing natural materials to build small, simple structures where we can experiment with designs that actually support life rather than perpetuate harm.

The truck is a 1990 Dodge Cummins bought for $4,000 and completely rebuilt. The pizza oven was designed by me and built by a Czech fabricator living in Port Townsend, Washington.

We have gone on to design more lightweight, more efficient, and cheaper ovens.

Shortly after moving to Port Townsend to farm, I met Chris Brady, who has been fundamental in nurturing my rambling pizza dream and teaching me how to build things other than skateboard ramps.

He managed the project, did the woodwork, did the design, and hired Andy Lillibridge from Eugene, Oregon to do the flatbed, steel frame, aluminum awnings, tables, etc. Because of the generosity and resourcefulness of all those involved in this slow-moving dream, rebuilding the truck and making the pizzeria cost under $25,000.

My background: I grew up on Lenni-Lenape land around Newark, New Jersey, listening to Tupac, skateboarding, and trying to figure out how to love myself and those around me when my surroundings made that next to impossible.

"…a wood-burning pizza truck that feeds people on the Olympic Peninsula in Washington"

"It's a truck, it's a kitchen, it's a dream, it's a home, it's science fiction."

Luckily, music and the skateboarding community kept me grounded, or I might have turned to drugs, or worse, become an investment banker.

At 18, I went south to Charleston, South Carolina for college, where I studied political science and Spanish and fortified my deep love of learning, Latin America, and my deep distrust of authoritarian institutions that force us to live flattened versions of ourselves.

In school, I spent time in Chile, and afterwards, went back to practice the tenets of magical realism that had inspired me. Hitchhiking, permaculture, and learning the history of the indigenous communities that, despite generations of oppression, continue to live resilient, beautiful lives that coexist with the earth.

This brought me to Washington state, where I've now lived for over a decade. I built a house out of reclaimed wood (including wood from the San Francisco Golden Gate Bridge toll booths) in the sticks of the Olympic Peninsula, scraping by on odd jobs, farming, cooking pizza, and trusting the great unknown.

"I guess most of all, it's a living commitment to building a more harmonious world."

Note from photographer Daniel Burgess:

The photos hopefully convey the many uses and setups possible with Mark's truck. Starting with the interior sleeping setup, then the exterior, fold-out awnings, pizzeria-in-action (sleeping setup removed), and then finally the rainproof canvas wrap (inside and out).

 instagram.com/mark_ennis_
www.flutterbypizzapie.com

Jay Nelson

I've been following builders for some 50 years now. I've got my favorites, as you can see in my books. Lloyd House, Louie Frazier, Bill Castle, Bruno Atkey, SunRay Kelley, Mark Hansen — unheralded master builders.

Lately it's occurred to me to do a book called Young Builders: The Next Generation. *If I do, first on my list will be Jay Nelson.*

Jay's an artist, a designer, and a master —

Rachel and me with daughters Romy and Zinnia. **Toyota Tacoma 04-19** *with aluminum flatbed, redwood frame, rigid foam, and fiberglass. Recycled sailcloth tent. This was my second pop-top, I got into doing pop-tops because I like the way you can store away your sleeping space. Photo by Aya Muto*

of concept, design, and construction.

He's built cabins, treehouses, three boats, designed restaurants, converted a San Francisco home into a duplex (See pp. 174–177, Small Homes*) and is now building a small home out of used wood on the Hawaiian island of Molokai.*

As sort of a sideline, he's built maybe 15 homes on wheels. He works in all materials: wood, metal, fiberglass, glass, canvas, copper; and his output is tremendous.

I find that everything he does to be a delight — this guy is having fun!

Sooner or later, there will be book on Jay.

Here, Jay writes about these nomadic creations.

—LK

MY GOAL IS TO BUILD SOMETHING that is light and functional and fits into my every day motions of life, while also having the right lines and shapes. They're rough, handmade structures. I do it for fun, I start with a rough idea, but then move past that. I enjoy the process of learning what it will be through building. The vehicle rethinks are special side projects to me, I generally don't build them for clients.

www.jaynelsonart.com
instagram.com/jaynelsonstudio

Dodge Cummins 92-14 *designed and built for Patagonia's Worn Wear recycled clothing operation. I had Precision Welding in Oroville weld the frame. Recycled redwood wine barrel, tongue-and-groove walls. Photo by Erin Feinblatt. (See* **shltr.net/jaywornwear**.)

Rachel and me with our **Honda CRX 92-06**, *poplar plywood and fiberglass. My first vehicle rethink. I made it to drive across the country and then to Nova Scotia and back. I'm often motivated by a trip I want to make and the vehicle that would suit that trip.*

2018 Hilux built in Bangalow / Byron Bay, NSW, Australia with Vissla surf gear in 10 days, made of Paulownia wood and fiberglass. Once built, we drove, surfed, and camped down the coast to Sydney, with help from Dana Burns Watson. We built it at Dana's shop on a chicken ranch. Photo by Jeremiah Klein

Toyota Previa AWD 94-20 with redwood and fiberglass, recycled sail tent, built for Marcos Mafia travel gear during the lockdown of 2020. I did a step-by-step online class with Inspire Courses on how to build a pop-top.

Mercedes 407D, below center. I built this one in Biarritz, France in 2016 and then drove it through Spain — surfing and camping with Rachel and Romy. Often when I travel to do these projects, I have a limited amount of time, usually 10 to 15 days. The goal is to come up with a simple plan that I can finish, while also making something that is aesthetically right and functional. It had two beds and a kitchen. Our larger bed converted into a dining area. For the roof I built a press (a skateboard technique) and the laminated ¼″ × 2″ stock to create curved framing. This is how I do all of my curves unless they're really tight. All the wood is local, except for the recycled windows and roofing. The flatbed is a really easy starting point because you have a flat square foundation ready to go. It was always my dream to build a '60s-type house truck, and this was definitely the more minimalist version of something like that.

More…

Suzuki SJ410 83-16

Lumber and copper. Built at Foster Huntington's in Washington with Lane Walkup. We built this in two weeks for a film Foster made called Micro Machine. (**shltr.net/copper**)

Foster's treehouses are in the images below and left.

Subaru Brat 86-18

*Acronym for "**B**i-drive **R**ecreational **A**ll-terrain **T**ransporter." A 4×4, built with the support of Subaru USA. Cedar and fiberglass, copper roof, recycled sail tent from Marcos Mafia, woodstove made from an ammunitions case (bought from Etsy). This still is my favorite rethink. The inside is spacious and comfortable, yet it packs up for a very small lightweight load. The only problem is that it's a two-seater. I built the Tacoma (see p. 132) after this because I needed a vehicle that could accommodate my two kids. Photos by Brian Flaherty*

Freedom on Wheels

Andy's 1986 Tacoma Turbo 4×4

Andy Diemer

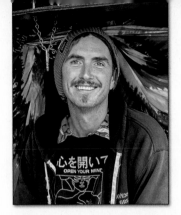

In June 2021, I spotted this unique rig parked in town and shot a photo. Its owner wasn't around, so I couldn't find out anything about it.

I posted it on Instagram the next day and was inundated with comments and likes. It was ultimately viewed by 23,000 people, and to this date is the most popular photo I've ever posted (out of some 1,600 posts). Something was going on here.

Several months later, the truck reappeared in town, and this time I met Andy, its creator and owner. Since then, I've met up with him half a dozen times and he's visited me at home. Each time I see him, the truck is different, as he's continually adding decorations and improving utility.

"Now every day is better and better. I'm so happy."

Andy was born in Flint, Michigan, moved to Lake Tahoe about 20 years ago and got into serious snowboarding. Then he lived in Bali for a while, then in a palapa on the beach in Costa Rica for $200 a month (la pura vida!).

Six months later, he moved back to Tahoe and lived in a cave on the east shore for three months, working as a sushi chef at night. Then back to Michigan, where he bought the truck in 2013, got some free lumber, and built the camper shell in his dad's garage.

From there, he moved to Key West, which he says is the number one spot for vans in the U.S., but he couldn't afford it, so he hit the road.

"Now every day is better and better. I'm so happy."

Andy has a contractor's license and works as a house painter. He figures he can survive for a year by working for four months.

He's also a poet.

The truck is a virtual magnet. Anywhere he parks, he's quickly surrounded by people. When he comes out from shopping in a market,

there will be four or five people standing around the truck, and he passes out his painting cards. He says women universally love the plants (which stay in place as he travels).

"I didn't have to look for a tribe; they found me."

It may not be noticeable at first, but the truck is immaculate. He is continually building and improving things. The sleeping nook in the upper story is cozy, with windows on three sides; it's like sleeping outside while staying dry.

"The universe had me build this."

The motor runs like clockwork. He's continually adding little touches, like the bamboo detailing, the ship's steering wheel at top front, little icons, paintings, plants....

Andy is one of the happiest and contented people I've ever met — and this makes other people happy. He radiates energy and charm, and loves life on the road.

"The freedom is unbelievable."

–LK

 Email: *andrewdiemerpuravida@gmail.com*

VITAL STATISTICS

- **Vehicle:** 1986 Toyota Tacoma 22RTE 2.4L 4×4
- **Motor:** CT-26 turbo from Toyota Supra
- **Generator (for occasional use):** Ryobi 2300 starting watts, 1800 running watts
- **Camper build:** Wood from pallets, bamboo—just about everything—was free.
- **Suspension:** Airbags with an extra leaf
- **Conveyances:** First-generation Laird Hamilton paddleboard he got for $200, a paddle, a skateboard, and a bike (and sometimes a motorbike).
- **Extras:** Too numerous to list

"The universe had me build this."

Bamboo detailing

More...

Our book, Shelter, *has won some space.*

Bedroom on top deck (see interior at right).

"I didn't have to look for a tribe; they found me."

Andy and his mom

Bedroom is cozy, has views all around.

"The freedom is unbelievable."

The Redwood Road Boat
Ben Bloom

"Inspiration for the camper's design was largely drawn from old wooden boats."

I'VE ALWAYS BEEN A BIT OF A HOMEBODY, but also love to be on the road. Campers represent the best of both worlds for me: the ability to travel and experience new places without giving up the feeling of comfort I associate with home.

For years I have been fascinated with mobile shelters of all kinds and often fantasized about one day having my own. When I was ready to invest in a camper, I spent a lot of time thinking about what type of vehicle would best suit my needs functionally.

I knew I wanted the camper to be capable enough off-road to take me to remote places, and also be reliable and maneuverable enough to drive daily. Ultimately, a small truck camper seemed like the best choice, and I was excited by the notion of being able to build my own.

Inspiration for the camper's design was largely drawn from old wooden boats, which I've long appreciated for their craftsmanship and whimsicality.

The shell is built entirely from California redwood, which is known for its natural beauty and weather resistance. The roof is covered with copper sheet metal, and the windows are antique portholes that were salvaged from a retired ship. The exterior is coated with marine-grade clear fiberglass and varnish, which provide protection from the elements and give the redwood a fittingly nautical appearance.

I have often found myself admiring how efficiently boat builders utilize interior space and how cozy the tiny cabins of boats can feel; I wanted this to be reflected in my camper's interior.

I built a platform over the wheel wells to support a queen-size mattress and a slide-out kitchen that fits underneath — which makes for easy food preparation and storage. The interior is completely modular, so I can add or remove the platform and kitchen easily, allowing more room for cargo whenever I need it.

Having a home away from home gives me a sense of comfort and ease wherever I go, and allows me to focus on the best parts of travel and exploration. The feeling of climbing into the back of the camper in the evenings is tough to beat, and I am excited to spend many more nights in my little road boat.

"The shell is built entirely from California redwood."

"Having a home away from home gives me a sense of comfort and ease wherever I go."

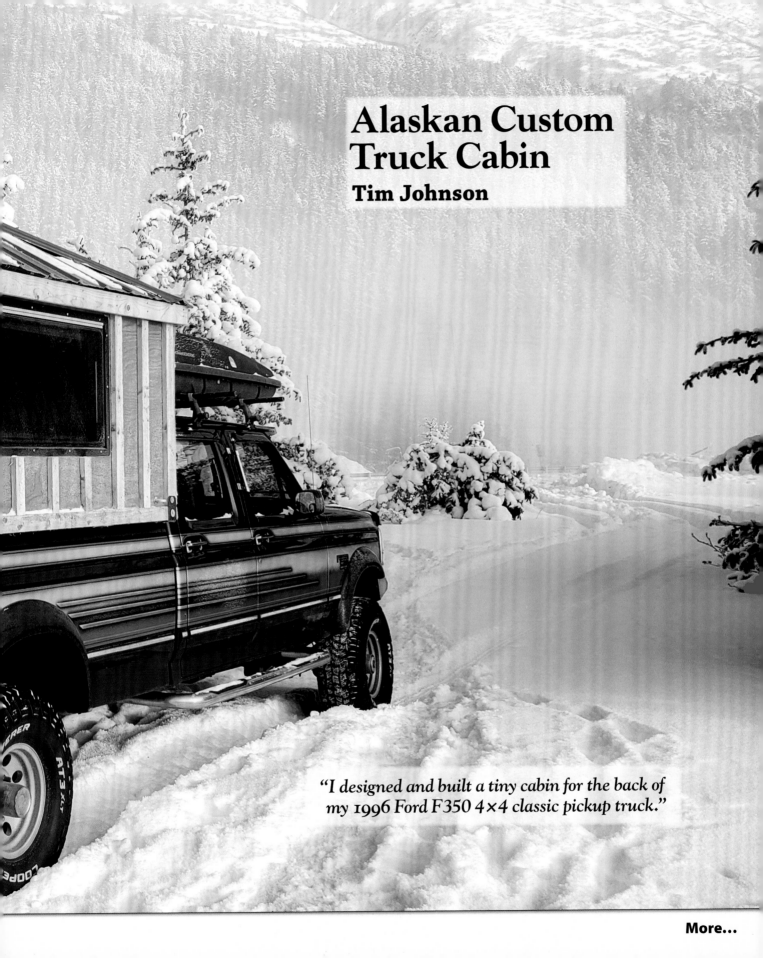

Alaskan Custom Truck Cabin

Tim Johnson

"I designed and built a tiny cabin for the back of my 1996 Ford F350 4×4 classic pickup truck."

More...

My DREAM OF LIVING IN THE WILDEST PLACE ON EARTH led me to Alaska. Inspired by summers spent building and living at my father's remote, no-road-access cabin, I moved from Georgia to Alaska in 2002.

As a senior in the Outdoor Studies program at Alaska Pacific University, I proposed writing a new river guidebook. In 2007, I wrote and self-published *Alaska Whitewater: A Guide to Rivers & Creeks in the Last Frontier.*

In 2012, I got tired of moving from apartment to apartment, so I flew to California and bought a 1989 Toyota Odyssey 4×4 motorhome and committed to living on the road in Alaska full-time, which I did for six years, until I could build my own log cabin with my Dad.

In 2018, I sold my beloved Toyota motorhome and built a 16′×20′ cabin with my Dad. With the leftover lumber from the cabin, I built the truck cabin shown here, and this led to starting a YouTube channel called *Full Send Alaskan Overland*, documenting my weekly adventures in the truck house.

I have been making whitewater kayaking videos on YouTube since 2007 but began taking filming more seriously in 2020, and it has made for quite the adventure!

I also started a custom cabin camper building business known as Coldfoot Campers here in Alaska, where I build custom cabin campers for a truck or trailer.

VITAL STATISTICS

Truck

- 1996 Ford F350 4×4 pickup truck, classic old-body style
- 7.3L Power Stroke turbo-diesel engine (one of the most reliable engines ever made)
- 180,000 mi. on the truck

Camper

- Handmade and self-designed with spray foam insulation for extremely cold winter camping in the Arctic
- Dometic 3-burner propane range and oven
- Dometic CC electric fridge/freezer under the couch
- Hand-pump faucet and 7 gal. portable water jug for simple, low-maintenance water needs
- Camco portable toilet (rolls out from under woodstove)
- Kimberly woodstove
- Dometic 16,000 BTU propane furnace for auxiliary/quick heat
- 100W Renergy solar panel on the metal roof
- Overland Pros outdoor shower enclosure awning, and an awesome covered front porch to sit out of the rain/sun.

I wouldn't do anything differently, as I spent quite a long time designing everything exactly the way I wanted it. If you want to build your own camper, I suggest thinking carefully about what you want to use the camper for, and build out your design based on what features and amenities you will actually use often. If you follow that advice, you will more than likely be very happy with your final product.

More...

www.youtube.com/c/TruckHouseLife
instagram.com/truckhouselife
coldfootdcamper@gmail.com

"I have been making whitewater kayaking videos on YouTube since 2007."

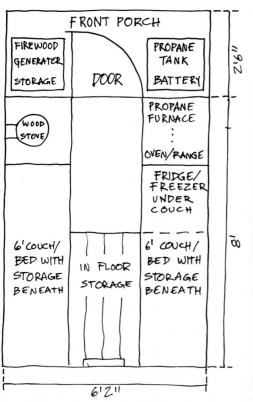

FRONT PORCH

| FIREWOOD GENERATOR STORAGE | DOOR | PROPANE TANK BATTERY |

WOOD STOVE

PROPANE FURNACE

OVEN/RANGE

FRIDGE/ FREEZER UNDER COUCH

6' COUCH/ BED WITH STORAGE BENEATH | IN FLOOR STORAGE | 6' COUCH/ BED WITH STORAGE BENEATH

2'9"

8'

6'2"

Tacoma TRD Cedar Camper

Ian Azariah

Photo: J. Kelsey

THE IDEA OF BUILDING A CUSTOM CAMPER ON THE BACK of my truck had been kicking around in my head for a while. After moving from a Toyota 4Runner to a Tacoma, I missed the ability to use my vehicle as a mobile headquarters in which I could travel, sleep, and basically live on the road without having to worry about the details.

After prowling the internet and being inspired by books like *Tiny Homes on the Move* and artists like Jay Nelson, everything lined up perfectly to make it happen. First I found a truck with a solid frame and low KM to build on, then a space next to my studio freed up, giving me a place to build.

I knew exactly what I was aiming to build right from the start, but what I did not know *yet* was how to build something that complicated. I had built other unconventional structures before: skate ramps, tree houses, mobile darkrooms, etc. But I had never built something as technically complicated as what I was undertaking.

My girlfriend Denise and I had most of the sub-frame done when my carpenter friend, Colin D. Watt, offered to come and help me out as things were getting very complicated quickly. Altogether, it took the three of us about four nonstop months of construction, research, problem-solving, and reconstruction to put the whole thing together.

The build finished the same day we took off on a two-week road trip around British Columbia. We had no particular plan other than to drive roads we had never been on and try and hit a hot spring or two along the way.

The camper worked flawlessly the whole trip and provided a huge increase in the smiles per gallon we got out of the truck. I was often approached by people wanting to chat about the camper, asking about the building process.

Most people asked if I designed and built it myself. I think the best part is seeing others get inspired by it and realize that they could make something like it too. And I hope they do.

"I had never built something as technically complicated as what I was undertaking."

www.ianazariah.com
www.tintypetrike.com
instagram.com/ianazariah
instagram.com/tintypetrike
instagram.com/ontheroadwithroscoe

"The estimated weight of the camper is around 600 pounds."

More...

Make: Toyota

Model: Tacoma TRD Off-Road

Engine: 3.4L V6

Year of vehicle: 2004

Mileage: 280,000 km

Suspension mods: RideRite air bags (rear)

The cap is constructed using 2×4s and a laminated plywood exoskeleton, then covered with ½″ bead-and-cove cedar planks. The windows are all segmented rings with plexiglass. It is finished with 6-ounce fiberglass and clear epoxy resin for waterproofing (like a boat or canoe). It has no stove, kitchen, or amenities, and is very simple.

Platforms can extend over the truck bed so you can sleep up top with your head in the crown of the camper, or you can set up the bed down below for more headroom. There is ample storage under the benches, which run the length of the truck bed. Keeping the build lightweight was one of my primary goals. The estimated weight of the camper is around 600 pounds.

Above: Facing cab
Below: Facing back of truck

What info can you pass along to people building or outfitting a vehicle?

Simply learn as you go, and don't be afraid to ask for help. Also, YouTube was a great resource for me.

I time-lapsed my whole build on my Instagram: **@ianazariah** in hopes it helps others.

What would you do differently if you had it to do over again?

I would try and draw the crown of the truck with a 3D program and get the plywood CNC cut to help make the lineup simpler. The crown was incredibly difficult to build. In addition, I did have to go back and fiberglass the outside of my lower windows, which open, in order to ensure they would not crack over time.

"The best part is seeing others get inspired by it and realize that they could make something like it too. And I hope they do."

4WD Toyota Tacoma Camper

Garrett Remde

Photos by Nate Duffy, Brandon Haley, and Garrett Remde

I made the bed and folding section, and the slats are from an old Ikea bed frame that a friend was throwing out.

Being a 20-something guy doing my best to roam, I feel like I rarely find people who want to make things themselves, let alone make every single part of something. I think that's the coolest thing possible. It forces you to think not only about how what you make will be used, but about what can complement and enhance it.

Granted, I didn't make every single nut and bolt that went into the thing, but I think I got pretty close. I haven't lived in it full-time yet, but the plan is in the works.

I feel it has most everything I need and has led me to meet loads of rad people at every stage of the build. Be it for waves, snow, or just getting out of town, I enjoy having a little cabin to drive around with.

> *"The idea for this camper came from a video I saw highlighting Jay Nelson's work."*

THE IDEA FOR THIS CAMPER CAME from a video I saw highlighting Jay Nelson's work. *(See pp. 132–135.)* I've followed his builds for a long time, always wanting to try something similar. He talks about building a camper with a trip or activity in mind, and so began the process of attempting to build my own surf and snowboard adventure vehicle.

I'm originally from California and very fortunate to have access to a well-equipped shop. The camper was built between there and my carport in Corvallis, Oregon, where I was attending school. I started building around Christmas 2019 by welding a steel frame and wrapping it in ⅜-inch plywood.

The exterior is wrapped in Grace Ice and Water Shield and topped with a galvanized steel sheet roof. The rest of the exterior was done in my carport in Oregon, and all the cedar was cut and installed with a hand saw and drill. It looks like I went crazy with screws because I did.... That's all I really had access to.

I made just about every piece of the camper myself. The three windows were built out of mahogany scraps from another project and fitted with plexiglass.

There are four brackets I made and carriage-bolted into the frame, which are for removing the camper with a hoist.

On the driver's side are custom J brackets to hold two surfboards.

The exterior is finished off with an 1880s era Sargent & Co. mortise lock; for this I made a wooden housing and receiver.

My father and I milled all the redwood siding for the interior in the Santa Cruz Mountains. It houses a homemade woodstove, kitchen storage cabinet, and various hangers and shelves.

I made almost all of my cooking utensils and restored a set of Wagner cast iron pans that I keep in the camper.

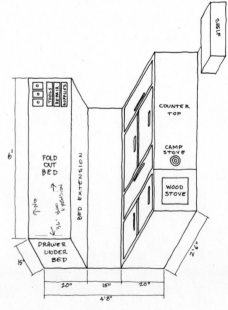

> *"It has most everything I need and has led me to meet loads of rad people."*

VITAL STATISTICS

Truck:
- 1999 Toyota Tacoma SR5
- 3.4L V6 engine with 260,000 mi.
- 5-speed manual transmission, 4WD
- Fabtech 6″ lift
- Air Lift rear air bag kit
- Addicted off-road plate bumper
- 15a Pro Comp alloy wheels
- 33/12.50/15 BFG K02 tires

Camper:
- Completely insulated and waterproof
- Locking mechanism made from 1880s-era Sargent & Co. mortise lock
- Approx. twin-size foldout bed
- Single-burner propane stove in camper / full-size camp stove stored in cabinet
- Storage for two surfboards inside and two outside on custom rack
- Self-made wood stove (chimney not yet installed)
- 3× windows (cab-thru and others yet to be installed)
- Gear / cooking storage in kitchen cabinet / cab-over
- Under-bed drawer holds 7 gal. water jug/tools
- Cheap fridge/cooler that plugs into outlet in truck cab

Future Plans:
- Cab-thru window
- 2× more DIY porthole windows
- Chimney for woodstove
- Solar
- DIY awning

"I made just about every piece of the camper myself."

The rear airbags were installed after I first put the camper on the truck. With its high center of gravity, it had quite a bit of body roll when going around corners. The bags stiffened the suspension and made it a much nicer daily driver. I'd definitely recommend installing something similar if putting a camper on the back of a compact pickup like the Tacoma with otherwise stock suspension. Mine has never been much of a trail rig so I don't mind the loss of articulation...until I need it of course.

Two Camper Shells by a German Carpenter

Tim Behnke

I BOUGHT A FORD TRANSIT PICKUP (2.2 TDCI 2010), intending to turn it into a camper, but also to use in my work as a carpenter. I was 23 years old when I started building the first one, and was still in a German carpentry school, so I just had time to work on the weekends.

It took me about nine months to finish the first camper (*photos on this page*). I saved money by using a lot of the wood scraps from the timber company I worked for.

After finishing the first truck camper, I couldn't sit still. I love to plan projects and create structures, so I decided to build another wooden home for my Ford Transit. Also, the camper was really heavy, not getting good gas mileage, and a bit awkward with such a heavy load.

I detached the camper from the truck, mounted three wooden studs on each side, and deflated the tires to get enough room between the camper and truck, so that I could then drive the truck out from under the camper.

For my new project, I wanted something smaller (*photos on opposite page*) so that there is enough room to take tools and building materials with me when I'm working on the road.

I wanted something that was big enough for me, yet as small as I could imagine. I still wanted to have a comfortable double bed, a space to cook meals, storage, and a small woodstove.

I wanted to use wood for construction and as few non-natural materials as possible.

For the roofing sheet, which had to be light and easy to maintain, I chose an old German truck tarp sheet. The end result is that I have a perfect work truck, as well as a camper for exploring nature, skating, and surfing. (I now go camping regularly.)

It gets about 10 kilometers per liter of diesel (about 24 miles per gallon).

The larger first shell is now used as a tool shed.

instagram.com/timbenkearth

Above, first truck; on next page, second truck

"I was 23 years old when I started building the first one, and was still in a German carpentry school."

"I wanted something smaller so that there is enough room to take tools and building materials with me when I'm working on the road."

"The end result is that I have a perfect work truck, as well as a camper for exploring nature, skating, and surfing."

Mikey's Snowchaser #2
Mike Basich

More...

Mike is a whirlwind of energy. It's hard to believe all he's accomplished in his life so far. World-class snowboarder, designer, builder, carpenter, welder, communicator and — underlying it all — seeker of adventure. He's also one of the rare builders who can translate his dreams into physical reality.

Mike has been in our last three books: Tiny Homes (where his unique mountain retreat is the first home in the book), Tiny Homes on the Move (his Snowchaser Dodge Ram truck with snowboard on roof), and Small Homes (his home in the Sierra foothills using milled on-site lumber).

Mike was hit with double disaster in the past year. His large workshop/warehouse/studio in Colfax, California, and later his home in Nevada County, were destroyed by separate fires. There was no fire insurance on the workshop, but with the help of a GoFundMe relief fund set up by a neighbor, he's been working nonstop to rebuild.

Here's Mike's most recent build. He says it's his fifth camper build, designed to fit inside a parking spot, to be homey inside, and to avoid the linear feeling with the clam shell, which opens sideways.

On a trip in 2017, he put it on a ferry from Bellingham, Washington to Haines, Alaska, where he met a snowboarder friend and they went snowboarding in a pass 30 miles outside of Haines.

 instagram.com/mikebasich
www.241collection.com

VITAL STATISTICS

- **Vehicle:** 2012 Mitsubishi Fuso FG Canter
- **Cabin frame:** 120-gauge 1″×2″ metal tubing
- **Exterior siding:** 26-gauge untreated cold-rolled steel over Owens Corning titanium UDL 30 peel-and-stick sheets of underlayment as waterproofing
- **Windows:** Home Depot stucco aluminum windows
- **Inside wood siding:** Custom-built ¼″ plywood birch wall paneling over silver bubble wrap insulation; ceiling is cedar T&G.
- **Walls** are 2″ thick, with 22R rating
- **Total length of vehicle:** 19′
- **Cabin weight:** 2,500 lbs.
- **Motor:** 3.0 diesel, 12 mpg.
- **Sleeping:** Two-in-one bed
- **Drive 2- or 4-wheel drive:** 4×4 manual locking hubs, 6-speed auto with Tiptronic shifting option
- **Suspension:** Stock
- **Awning:** Passenger side of cabin opens like a clam shell, providing shade for a deck, plus shelter from sun or rain.
- **Solar electricity:** Goal Zero 100W solar panel; deep-cycle Morningstar auxiliary batteries; 2,000W inverter
- **Jumper cables, tow ropes, tire pumps, traction.** With the insulator charging system, from alternator to auxiliary batteries, pushing a button will jump start the motor if truck's batteries go dead.
- **Water:** 40 gal. of fresh water in plastic tank inside to avoid freezing
- **Water heating:** On-demand propane water heater; pipes under floor to sink and bathtub
- **Air heater:** Williams direct-vent heater runs on no electricity, thermostat-controlled, 10-gallon propane tank.
- **Ventilation fan:** 12-volt, 1-speed fan for ceiling, super quiet
- **Kitchen:** 16″ slide-out; sliders are custom made but run on 12V remote controlled actuators.
- **Cooking:** 2 burners and oven for cooking run off small propane tank. Burner and oven can be moved outside for outdoor cooking.
- **Refrigerator:** 12V Isotherm fridge makes ice, runs on two 6V batteries charged from 100W solar panels.
- **Bed** turns into dining table.
- **Heat:** Wood-burning stove for heat and cooking; attached to swinging door so it can be swung outside for outdoor cooking.
- **Tommy tailgate** tucks under or serves as deck.
- **Top speed:** 80 mph.
- **Storage** compartments under floor

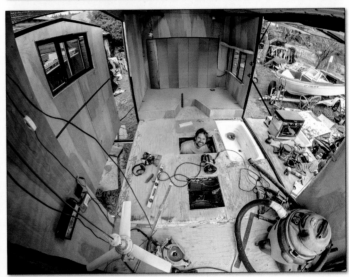

More...

"Passenger side of cabin opens like a clam shell, providing shade for a deck, plus shelter from sun or rain."

"Designed to fit inside a parking spot, to be homey inside, to avoid the linear feeling with the clam shell, which opens sideways."

The Lorry Life
Tom Duckworth

"I have lived in the truck full-time for three years."

Sango Bay, near the village of Durness, in the nothwest Scottish Highlands

More...

*"Two weeks after I bought the
base vehicle for £4350, I lost my job."*

A COMBINATION OF MY LOVE FOR old vehicles, ambition to build my own home in a sustainable way, and desire to travel inspired this project. Four years on, I have lived in the truck full-time for three years, and it's taken us on some amazing adventures, including around Scotland to complete the NC500 (*a 500-mile tour of the northern coast of Scotland*), Yorkshire, Wales, Cornwall, and the New Forest.

Plans for future trips include going around the Baltic Sea, south Europe, and Africa, and we're already planning the next overlanding build to take us further afield, but more on that later....

The vehicle is a 1988 Bedford MJ ex-British army truck. The living space is 8m² (86 sq. ft.) — which includes a kitchen, bathroom, and sitting room — and is below the "bedroom."

The kitchen includes a worktop made from the original truck bed wood, a bottle-top splash behind the Belfast sink, a three-burner Thetford oven, a 40-liter (42-quart) Dometic refrigerator/freezer, and cupboards made from repurposed ammo crates.

The bathroom consists of a rainwater shower and compost toilet, surrounded by metro tiles. The sitting room's main feature is a Chesterfield sofa, which sits below maps for planning adventures.

Above this is a double bed, which lowers down on a pulley system. Also on a pulley system is the beer terrace, which lowers to sit above the cab; this wouldn't be complete without a beer pump or 'The Pub,' which is fixed on the back of the truck.

The rig is also complete with a 4-kilowatt wood burner, Crittall steel windows, LPG instant boiler, 360-liter (95-gallon)

rainwater collection tank, 720-watt solar panels, and a 240 Ah leisure battery.

The engine is 5.4L multi-fuel, and the total mileage is unknown, as the army had the odometer disconnected. However, I've done over 10,000 miles, with all 9.5 tons, no power steering, and the steering wheel on the wrong side for the United Kingdom.

With the truck being such an old vehicle, I've had to roll my sleeves up and fix a fair few mechanical hiccups along the way. One of the main questions we get asked is miles per gallon; for now it's about 11, but we prefer to think of it as smiles per mile.

Initially I thought the build would take half a year, but with a 40- to 60-hour work week, it took 14 months.

Two weeks after I bought the base vehicle for £4350, I lost my job, meaning

I also lost my build space, storage, and income. The help of a good friend (Makkai) got me through this and allowed me to continue with my plan.

The build wasn't easy and at the time was the most challenging thing I'd done, but even taking snowy bucket showers off the back of the truck during a particularly harsh winter wasn't enough to make me regret the choice I'd made.

Building the habitation pod structure—including frame, recycled pallet cladding, and roof—was by far the most challenging aspect and something I'd strongly encourage anyone to consider carefully before embarking upon. However, taking a step back and seeing what I'd built for the first time made every bit of it worthwhile.

I've since built a matching trailer workshop and I am now following my dream: building customized camper vans and overlanders for a living. To see my biggest project yet, check out my Instagram accounts and blogs. *(See below.)*

Once these projects are done and we are ready, we plan to build another overlanding rig to take us traveling around the whole world. We can't wait.

"I am now following my dream: building customized camper vans and overlanders for a living."

 Instagram:
    instagram.com/the_lorrylife
    instagram.com/duckworthoverland

   Blogs:
    www.thelorrylife.com
    www.duckworthoverland.com

More...

*Bed
elevated
via pulley
system*

Bed lowered

"I've done over 10,000 miles, with all 9.5 tons."

"I like to be unruly in this world.
We need to lead creative lives and have fun!"

Le Benne-Benz

Yogan Carpenter

Yogan first appeared in our books with his tree house in Tiny Homes *(pp. 154–155), then again with his van that hooked up to a cabin in* Tiny Homes on the Move *(pp. 18–19).*

He is an incredibly prolific and imaginative carpenter and designer. Here he and a few of his friends are back with their latest creations.

(He is presently translating our book Shelter *for publication in France.)*

–LK

AFTER SELLING MY MERCEDES Sprinter 311 CDI extra-long van *(see Tiny Homes on the Move, pp. 18–19)*, I bought a 2002 411 CDI Mercedes Sprinter van with a double cab (seven seats) and a hydraulic bed lifter.

I chose a seven-seat van because we live in the CopeauXcabana community, and it's really cool to go to festivals with only one van!

We can carry all our stuff (tent, mattress, table, portable hot tub, etc.) in the truck bed and we need only one driver. It's also perfect if you have more than one child in your family.

I bought this van because it's perfect for my work as a carpenter. The bed is 2 × 2.3 meters (6.6 × 7 feet) but I can carry beams up to 8 meters (26 feet) long. In addition, it's a good size for our hot tub, as well as a good stage for live music!

Now that I have a child, a girlfriend, and a cat, I wanted a cozy van. The idea to make a removable camper shell came during a discussion one day with my friend Martin.

When I travel, I like to take nude sunbaths and sleep under the stars, so I built a roof that opens.

I made 10 curved rafters by laminating eight layers of 9mm (⅜″) poplar; I then glued and screwed two layers of 6mm (¼″) plywood on: poplar plywood for the first layer and okoumé for the second. (I used two pieces of 6mm plywood rather than one because it's too difficult to bend 12mm in one operation.)

I used quite a few hinges, concealed in the laminated arches, so I can open the roof and sides in various configurations.

I can open the sides and rear drop side of the bed (with a chain system) to have 5m² (52 sq. ft.) more floor area, so I have a balcony, workbench, bar, and kitchen counter.

I painted it with Rephanol, a German rubber product, in a copper color because I like the oxidation of this material, from pink to blue and brown.

I have four metal feet with cranks, so I can lift the camper off the truck and leave it anywhere (and also level it simply). *(See next page.)*

If, after a week of working, we want to go to a festival or take a break in the country, it only takes 10 minutes to put the camper on the van and leave!

More...

"I can park on a slope of up to 50 degrees and still level the camper."

I can level the camper with the hydraulic bed, which is great because you can find many more good camping spots if the ground doesn't have to be level. I can park on a slope of up to 50 degrees and still level the camper.

Under the bed I have a lot of space for my paraglider, skateboard, accordion, Emily's hurdy-gurdy, Orso's wooden games, a lot of my *Cabanophiles* books to sell and exchange during travels, as well as a good carpentry toolbox for whatever projects I may run across.

After doing complicated light and music installations in my last three vans, I decided to make it simple here. I use my JBL Bluetooth speaker power bank connected to a nice LED light string and some USB-charging LED lamps.

I charge them, as well as my camera battery, on the 12-volt socket from the van while driving.

This camper cost me less than 600 Euros!

I travel often with Emily, my son Orso, and our cat Suzette. We plan to travel in Scandinavia, Romania, and Great-Britain.

When we're on the road. we meet people who live like us, on the road, or who live in unusual shelters, and we exchange experiences and compare our lives. Eventually I take pictures and do interviews for my next book.

Two of my friends in our community have vans like this; Martin made "La Boite-Mobile" on his Volkswagen T5 4×4 *(left in the picture),* and Alain made "The Ultra-Maçon Box" on his 1987 508d Mercedes! It's the future!

Using a van with a bed and removable camper is a good way to avoid complicated rules in France because now it's illegal to build your own rolling home. With this system, you can be creative!

I like to be unruly in this world. We need to lead creative lives and have fun!

There is always a solution.

www.cabanophiles.com
yogan.over-blog.com
instagram.com/yogancarpenter
facebook.com/yogancarpenter

"Now that I have a child, a girlfriend, and a cat, I wanted a cozy van."

"I bought this van because it's perfect for my work as a carpenter."

More...

"This camper (shell) cost me less than 600 Euros!"

"When I travel, I like to take nude sunbaths…

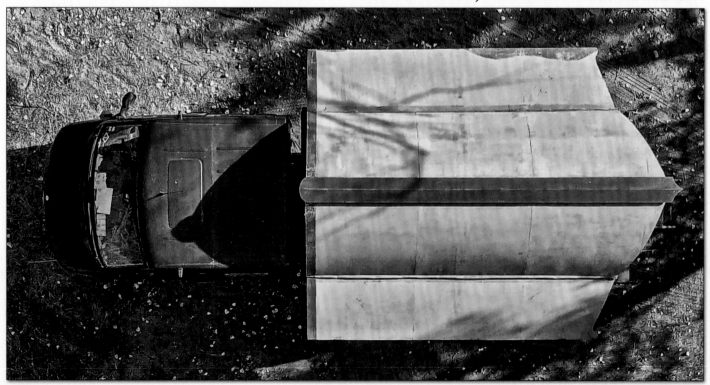

Camper parked in front of CopeauXcabana workshop, built in 2014 by Yogan and his carpenter friends in southwest France. They work mostly with oak and chestnut trees from the forest and use axes and a sawmill to make their timber frame (mortise and tenon) structures.

...and sleep under the stars, so I built a roof that opens."

See pp. 180–181 and 228–231 for three more rigs by Yogan and friends.

Canadian House Truck

Kai Watkins
Photos: Dylan Davies

I'VE ALWAYS BEEN INTO BUILDING THINGS. When I was a kid growing up on the kind of island featured in your *Builders of the Pacific Coast* book, we'd put together little driftwood forts down on the beach.

I was hugely inspired by that book: silvery driftwood, hand split shakes, things repurposed in creative ways. I wanted to build my own little unique wooden shack!

Finding the book *Some Turtles Have Nice Shells* provided the second inspiration. If I can't afford real estate, why not build my cabin on a truck?

The truck is a 1993 International, with a DT466 diesel engine, manual transmission, and hydraulic brakes. Everything is dead simple.

I wanted something that would be easy and cheap to fix. I tried to make it as organic-looking as possible, while still fitting in the maximum 8′ × 13.6′ × 32′ envelope.

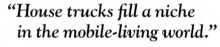

"House trucks fill a niche in the mobile-living world."

To accomplish that, I cut the ridge beam out of two 2 × 12s to have a gentle curve, and the cab-over sleeping loft has rounded corners. Originally I wanted the ridge to be a single log with a natural curve, but weight considerations must be made!

The house has a steel superstructure, with traditional wood studs fitted in between. The board-and-batten siding is cut thin, around ⅜″. The cedar shakes are all hand-split, mostly from driftwood.

The tail end of the truck is stepped down a foot, which gives more head room in the "conversation pit," as well as bringing the back deck lower.

The square windows are salvaged from a 100-year-old house, as are the floors, interior tongue and groove, and much of the hardware. I made the doors and the custom round window myself, and I etched my own designs into the antique brass doorknobs and keyhole covers.

We heat mostly with a small woodstove; cooking and water heating is done with propane, and we have a small 12-volt system with a single RV battery that is charged from shore power. Eventually I'd like to expand it, get solar panels, and charge the batteries from the sun as well as off the truck's alternator.

There's been a lot of collaboration with artists and artisans in my community; I consider myself lucky to be able to feature their work in the build.

It took me five years to get it to where I could lock it up, and as soon as it was weathertight, we moved in. No lights, plumbing, or insulation, but we had to take the plunge.

People always ask when I'll be finished, and I always answer "next summer." This rig is meant for moving to a location and hunkering down for a bit, rather than being constantly on the road.

House trucks fill a niche in the mobile-living world: bigger than a van, with a more flexible layout than a bus, more easily mobile than a tiny house. There's a lot of potential for creative builders to make something special.

Another good thing is that most heavy trucks are capable of carrying very heavy loads. (This one's max gross weight is 33,000 pounds!) Buses and vehicles towing house trailers cannot handle anything like this weight.

Although I did the majority of the work myself, I've had help from a wide range of people: family, friends, total strangers!

I've found that people are really supportive of someone doing things a little differently.

Blue and white tiles in the kitchen are by Simone Littledale; yellow and green tiles in the fireplace, by Mercury Mosaics; the woodstove is a Dwarf 4kW by Tiny Wood Stoves.

The front loft porthole has a funny story: Ben and I had been dating a couple of weeks when I asked him if he wanted to see me over the weekend. He said he couldn't because he was going wreck looting with his pirate draft-dodging Finnish friend. I thought, "OK, whatever. If you don't want to hang out, you don't have to make up some story," and sarcastically told him to bring me back a porthole as a gift.

He disappeared for two weeks. I heard nothing from him and thought, "Well, guess that's over," when one day he showed up at my door unannounced and said "Close your eyes." And —*thunk!*— drops this beautiful, huge porthole in my hands! I just about cried.

What a way to impress a girl! He had put on his scuba gear and pried it off a sunken boat especially for me.

Ben also got put to work on our fifth date splitting cedar

shakes from chunks of driftwood that I'd chainsawed and hauled to the building site. I don't think he knew what he was getting into when I asked if he wanted to help me build "just a small thing!"

"I've always been into building things."   **More…**

"I don't think he knew what he was getting into when I asked if he wanted to help me build 'just a small thing!'"

"I tried to make it as organic-looking as possible."

More...

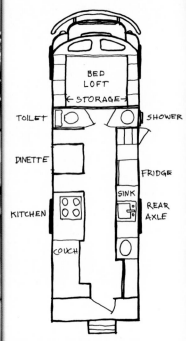

"*Most heavy trucks are capable of carrying very heavy loads.*"

"…an abandoned 1952 Dodge B3HH flatbed truck — a perfect floor!"

Mr Watts

Yogan Carpenter

In 2017, Yogan and his carpenter friend Menthé flew to California from France, stopping first here at Shelter Publications, and then hitchhiking up the coast to Vancouver Island, visiting a number of builders — some of whom had been featured in our book Builders of the Pacific Coast. *Here is Yogan's description of the trip.* —LK

ON OUR HITCHHIKING TRIP BETWEEN San Francisco and Vancouver Island, our idea was to meet some of the famous artistic builders of the Pacific Coast and, as well, offer to exchange our building skills for room and board.

After meeting Louie Frazier during a road trip with Lloyd Kahn, helping SunRay Kelley on his tree house, visiting the Salmon Creek farm community, and seeing Jan Janzen's gazebo in Tofino, British Columbia, we stayed with a lovely family in Humboldt County, in Northern California, and decided to build a crazy cabin.

At the bottom of the garden was an abandoned 1952 Dodge B3HH flatbed truck — a perfect floor!

We built a half-timber frame out of redwood, which was recovered from an old barn, as were the shingles. To get the curved roof, we cut the rafters from 10-inch-wide planks; each of the two parts was then inverted for the opposite sides. Then everything was screwed and glued together: a very economical and easy technique for an interesting result.

It took 10 days to build, faster than it would have been if we had done mortise-and-tenon joints. Everything was cut with a chainsaw and assembled with screws, a technique unfortunately very common in the U.S.A. The pegs are therefore only for looks!

This truck house, named Mr Watts, thanks to its old New York license plate, is 6 meters (20′) high, 9 meters (30′) long and 3.5 meters (11½′) wide. It's pretty lightweight, due to the use of redwood.

The rooftop and the stained glass window above the front door let light into the cabin. At the rear of the vehicle, the stairs fold into the platform that doubles as a workbench.

It's not designed to go on the road!

It was really fun to make Mr Watts and so good to work with old-growth redwood!

*"We built a half-timber frame out of
redwood recovered from an old barn."*

*"Everything was cut with a chainsaw
and assembled with screws."*

House Truck Built of Salvaged Materials

Derek "Deek" Diedricksen

Photos by Dylan Jon Wade Cox and Derek "Deek" Diedricksen

A LITTLE BACKSTORY ON THIS ONE: It's a full-time dwelling that I led the build/design on for a friend, Alex Eaves — reuse advocate/filmmaker/co-builder — in 2017.

The goal was to create a mobile tiny home (decor and all) with a large percentage of discarded, salvaged, and dumpster-dived materials (over 80% — easily).

The final decor and construction budget was under $800 as a result. This doesn't factor in the cost of the second-hand truck (around $8,000).

The 17-foot "box" of this former U-Haul moving truck now contains two sleeping levels, a small kitchen, a work desk area, and even a nautical-style wet bath (toilet and shower stall).

It's featured in a documentary film we made that shows the design process and shows viewers the "how," from start to finish. Because most of its materials are reused, there is a story, or lineage, in almost everything: plywood from an old concert sign, a ladder from an abandoned 1930s theater, spare drum set parts as drawer pulls, etc. People can head to **BoxTruckFilm.com** for more information and to check out the feature-length movie.

L-R: Derek, Alex

> *"The goal was to create a mobile tiny home (decor and all) with a large percentage of discarded, salvaged, and dumpster-dived materials."*

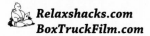
Relaxshacks.com
BoxTruckFilm.com

Deek's tiny house and tree house work can be found through *www.relaxshacks.com* or through his YouTube channel of the same name.

"The final decor and construction budget was under $800."

Building Bluebell

by Georjie Adams

BLUEBELL IS A HANDMADE HOME built on a chassis cab,* created with recycled, reclaimed, and donated materials, with the exception of the bespoke wood burner, hob (*cooktop stove*), and electrical system.

I started this building project because of the housing crisis, but also because I desperately wanted to find a slower, simpler, and lower-impact lifestyle — and not spend most of my life working to climb an outrageously overpriced housing ladder. Many people who seek alternative living feel the same way. Maybe where my back story differs is in two main things:

1. My absolute belief that anyone can build, regardless of training or experience. When I started building Bluebell, I could barely use a drill. I had absolutely no building skills and didn't know how a chisel worked.

Where I live and build (South Downs, England), I have no teacher, no wi-fi, and no mobile internet, so I've been on my own from the beginning.

I had no choice but to learn through feeling and intuition, relying heavily on my physical senses just as a child learns, and using the power of visualization for solving problems.

I was excited to learn that intuition alone — accompanied by not being afraid to make mistakes — is enough of a basis for using basic tools and materials.

When I had no idea where to start on the more involved engineering aspects of the project, I would shut my eyes and visualize hundreds of scenarios — how turning around a tight corner would put pressure on the wood joints, how strong storm-driven winds would stress the cladding, how speed bumps and deep potholes might loosen bolts, how water droplets streaming across the roof in the rain could cause leaks....

---

*Vehicle with just chassis rails and a cab

Learning to build this way often meant struggling to find very simple answers, and it also meant I often had doubts as to whether or not I was capable. But most importantly, I came to the stunning conclusion that with perseverance always comes a solution!

No power saw or electric drill could match the power of stubborn determination, the ultimate tool! Building almost entirely by hand with very few power tools left me feeling that we all have the ability to build.

Nothing has been better for my confidence, sense of self, perspective on the world, and mental health than learning how to use my two hands. Women are constantly told they aren't suited for hard physical labor, which leads me to:

2. The fight back against the sexism and misogyny in the building trades, which alleged that as a woman, I wouldn't be able to build my home myself, that no way would I be able to acquire construction skills equal to a man's.

It was an epiphany to learn that building — at least in fundamentals and everyday basics — was really simple! How had I been led to believe (through direct/indirect comments and, more problematically, deeply flawed ideology)

that this crucial life skill was so far out of reach that not only are women not as physically capable as men but not mentally capable of producing their own building plans? Everything I knew about building until that moment had reenforced a narrative that it's not a woman's place: that's just the way things are.

Encouraging eco building and natural craftsmanship is great, but I believe without a *big* effort to bring women to a level playing field and encourage building as a genderless endeavor, we won't make anywhere near enough progress to truly raise the potential of alternative living and climate-friendly building.

And that's not even taking into account the power that could extend to social mobility if women could have enough basic skills to fix a hinge on a cupboard or put up a shelf.

This is why I've started the website, *In Her Hands*, which aims to create an empowering space for women to learn and explore the fundamentals of construction. It will do this initially as an inspirational online platform with short films, podcasts, articles, and conversations with women builders, and ultimately grow into an organization providing physical workshops, events, and social outreach.

www.InHerHands.org
instagram.com/BuildingBluebell

"*Everything I knew about building until that moment had reenforced a narrative that it's not a woman's place.*"

> *"Building it almost entirely by hand with very few power tools..."*

VITAL STATISTICS

Vehicle:

- 2013 Iveco Daily cab, medium wheelbase
- **Mileage:** When bought, 60,000 mi.

Kitchen:

- Live-edge elm continuous kitchen worktop with lids for sink and hob made from same piece
- Two-ring gas hob *(cooktop stove)*
- Wood-burning stove with small oven compartment for cooking
- Victorian jam-making copper pot remade into sink, manual foot-pump water system — just cold water, nice and simple!
- Upcycled and restored old carved doors and ex-Georgian floorboards for siding
- Entirely upcycled ancillaries and brass fittings
- Two pull-out drawers and two large cupboard spaces with bin-saved rails and wheels
- Fridge under seat — big space saving for kitchen unit

Bathroom:

- Handmade composting toilet, all upcycled materials with 12V fan
- Large shower cubicle — separate space, not a wet room
- Hot water through underfloor-mounted Whale marine water heater

Bedroom and Living Space:

- Double bed in an overhead dome bedroom space with three windows (including an opening skylight and restored stained glass window)
- Upcycled cedar cladding, all handcut and sliced individually to accommodate dome curves
- Small reading light and one USB charger
- Large enough to sit up in bed fully with extra headroom

- **Electric:**
- 500W solar for most electric needs. 195A battery
- Inverter and main hook-up point
- Battery-to-battery charger for charging while engine is running
- 2 USB points, one 12V charging outlet, small battery display monitor and one double-socket 240V. Simple, but enough for me!

More...

*"Where I live and build (South Downs, England),
I have no teacher, no wi-fi, and no mobile internet."*

"No power saw or electric drill was a match for the
power of stubborn determination, the ultimate tool!"

A Rolling Home for Twelve Baby Bison

Luke Griswold-Tergis

Luke, a filmmaker, is one of the kindred spirits — as are Mike Basich (pp. 156–161), Foster Huntington (pp. 48–51), and Jay Nelson (pp. 132–135) — who have appeared in a number of our books.

A year or so ago, Luke sent me a photo of a no-nonsense Russian house truck. Upon further inquiry, it turned out that Luke was on another of his many life adventures — this time transporting a dozen baby bison through Siberia to a nature preserve in northeastern Siberia. Here is Luke's story.

—LK

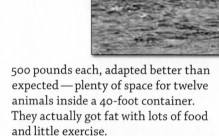

I PASSED THROUGH THE KOLYMA WITH Nikita Zimov and twelve baby bison. We were in transit from a farm in Denmark to Pleistocene Park — an unusual conservation and stave-off-the-apocolypse project in the far northeast corner of Siberia, almost to Alaska. We crossed most of two continents to get there, 11 time zones, six weeks on the road — drive, hay, water, shovel bison shit, sleep, drive....

We loaded the bison in the end of April. From Denmark across Germany, Poland, and Belarus, the bison traveled in a fancy Euro-livestock carrier.

At the border we were met by two Russian truck drivers, a vintage Mercedes semi pulling Nikita's custom luxury bison RV (shipping container with doors and air vents), and a Russian UAZ 4×4 pickup as a support car. (Nikita swore he would never buy a Russian-made vehicle, but he got a bit more patriotic when he discovered a brand new Russian truck was cheaper than a 20-year-old Toyota.)

We crossed European Russia, hitting the Volga in a late spring heat wave — not good for animals. Then the Ural Mountains — a bit anticlimactic as far as continent-defining ranges go. Officially in Siberia, we drove for several days through a swamp somewhere north of Kazakhstan — several hours of birch trees, a village, several more hours of birch.

The bison, yearlings, already weighing

500 pounds each, adapted better than expected — plenty of space for twelve animals inside a 40-foot container. They actually got fat with lots of food and little exercise.

Sometimes at night they would commence a wild rumpus. To the poor truck driver, trying to sleep in the cab, a tornado of little bison crashing into the walls of a container sounds and feels like an artillery barrage.

I first met Nikita six years earlier when I landed on his door step with a video camera and a plan to make a film about

him, his dad, and Pleistocene Park. The "participant observation" aspect of ethnographic film is a slippery slope. The film progressed slowly and over that time I got sucked more deeply into their project.

In Novosibirsk we had the best meal of the trip: *shashlik*, central Asian BBQ lamb, which Nikita's mother-in-law brought from Kyrgyzstan. Near Lake Baikal the scenery picked up. There was still ice along the shores of the lake. After the Republic of Buryatia (somewhere north of Mongolia) we split from the main road and turned north. The pavement ended.

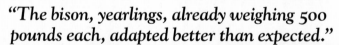

"The bison, yearlings, already weighing 500 pounds each, adapted better than expected."

"Sergey and his son Nikita are resurrecting the vanished ice age ecosystem in the most remote corner of Siberia."

Pleistocene Park was founded by Nikita's father, Sergey Zimov, in late Soviet times. Zimov the elder walks the fine line between madman and genius. Twenty years ago he rocked the scientific community by publishing a paradigm-shattering discovery in *Science* magazine: Frozen arctic soils contain twice as much carbon as the earth's atmosphere. These soils are starting to melt. This could make climate change virtually unstoppable.

Sergey proposed that millions of horses, bison, reindeer, yaks, muskoxen, camels — and perhaps cloned wooly mammoths — once again roaming the northern half of Asia, could stabilize permafrost and prevent a catastrophic scenario of runaway global warming.

Seeking no one's help and asking nobody's permission, Sergey and his son Nikita are resurrecting the vanished ice age ecosystem in the most remote corner of Siberia. They are scouring the planet for holdovers from the Ice Age and transporting them, by whatever low-budget means they can contrive, to Pleistocene Park — their landscape-scale experiment and proof-of-concept.

After Yakutsk, the coldest city on earth, we turned east again on the Kolyma highway — "highway" being a very generous term. On the globe we were somewhere north of Japan. Now the only other vehicles were big, gnarly Russian trucks.

More...

The Mercedes semi, built for the Autobahn and already worn out before it started this trip, started seriously disintegrating. In the first days of June, after another week crossing arctic mountain ranges, and winding through spent placer mines and abandoned ghost cities of the Kolyma gold fields, we made it to Seymchan, the village at the end of the last dirt road in Asia.

We loaded onto a river barge, pickup truck perched precariously on top of the bison container (great view), and set off north, down the Kolyma river. On the second day we got stuck on a sand bar, a dicey situation.

The upper part of the river is only navigable during the spring flood. With the water falling fast, we could have been there all summer. Nikita optimistically pointed out that we had a month of bison food and plenty of water. Unfortunately we had only a little more than a week's worth of human food. A passing tug boat pulled us off.

On day 36 we rammed the barge into a muddy river bank at Pleistocene Park. The workers at the park built a gangplank and Nikita chainsawed open the bisons' stalls. They nervously peered out of the container, eying their new home, then, all together, thundered down the gangplank and into Pleistocene Park. They milled about in a tight herd, then found some clumps of grass and started eating.

All the bison survived the trip. They are now three years old. This spring Nikita spotted two calves in the herd. Sergey Zimov calculates it will take about 10 million bison and another 10 million horses, reindeer, and muskoxen to keep permafrost frozen and avoid a catastrophic global warming feedback loop, so they still have a ways to go.

But there is progress. Nikita just brought Bactrian camels to the park and is currently working on a plan to bring more bison and muskoxen in the fall. George Church (Harvard geneticist) is advancing his plan to resurrect a wooly mammoth to aid Sergey and Nikita's mission. My documentary should be playing at film festivals about the same time that this book is published.

www.PleistoceneParkMovie.com
www.PleistocenePark.ru

"*They nervously peered out of the container, eying their new home, then, all together, thundered down the gangplank and into Pleistocene Park.*"

"We crossed European Russia, hitting the Volga in a late spring heat wave."

A tiny house on the move — Russian style — sighted along the "Road of Bones" through the Kolyma gold fields in northeast Siberia. (Bones referencing the Stalin-era prisoners who built it.) I honestly don't know much about the rig. The truck is a Ural 6×6, ubiquitous in this part of the world.

A Bus for All Seasons
Jonathan Paige and Stephanie Allan

More...

W E ONLY PLANNED ON LIVING IN the bus for one summer, but after putting so much love and sweat and into it, we knew we weren't going to be selling it any time soon.

We started the build in Taos, New Mexico, and "finished" it at my parents' place in Nardin, Oklahoma, with help from the family. Grandma made the seat cushions and all the curtains, and Dad's help was enlisted throughout. Total build time was just over two months.

We started our life in the bus by heading to Baja, picking up our friends Allie and Forrest along the way.

The bus was surprisingly comfortable for four people, and we spent over a month together surfing, kiteboarding, and eating tacos. People were genuinely curious about the bus and we had many visitors poke their heads in for a look (including a donkey).

We headed north after Baja. Even though the bus was built for the summer, it's true strength was in the snow. At Steph's request, we outfitted a diesel heater with modifications for a boot and glove dryer.

It allowed us to ski in comfort all over the Rockies and Cascades from New Mexico to British Columbia. That heater was easily the best addition (except maybe the hammock) to the bus. Quite often I would be inside wearing just shorts when the temperature was well below freezing.

Having worked ski seasons in the U.S.A. and New Zealand, we had many friends scattered throughout mountain towns in North America. Steph's sister Heidi and her partner Tom were able to join us for a month in Canada, and after some slight modifications to the "spare bed," we were all able to sleep warmly and comfortably. In fact, we were able to sleep five once when ski-touring Rogers Pass, BC.

In many places, we were happily snowed in; we had everything we needed to enjoy ourselves, including the occasional roast chicken.

The best part of the bus is being able to share it with so many people. Traveling to awesome places and hosting friends and family in something we were able to build ourselves (with lots of help from Dad) has created some of our best memories. Thanks for asking us to contribute to *Rolling Homes!*

In the Snow

"In many places, we were happily snowed in."

"We were able to sleep five once when ski-touring Rogers Pass, BC."

VITAL STATISTICS

- **Model:** 1998 International 3800 (Amtran conversion)
- **Engine:** T444E w/automatic transmission (220,000 mi.)
- **Fuel:** Diesel
- **Water Capacity:** 100L (26 gal.)
- **Heater:** Eberspacher Airtronic D5 (5kW) diesel heater
- **Refrigerator:** Dometic CFX95 / Yeti 65
- **Cooking:** Propane (stovetop & oven)
- **Solar:** 580W (Two 290W panels)
- **Battery:** 12V/370Ah (Two Trojan L16E-AC)
- **Electronics:** 12V DC & 110V AC
- **Bonus:** Bluetooth record player & soundbar

"Even though the bus was built for the summer, it's true strength was in the snow."

More...

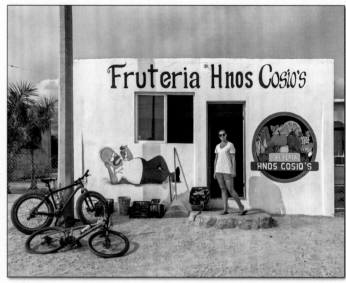

In Baja

"We spent over a month together surfing, kiteboarding, and eating tacos."

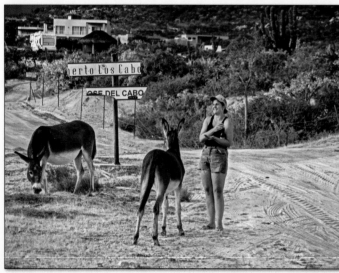

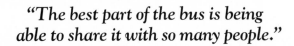

Looking toward the front of the bus (photo above)

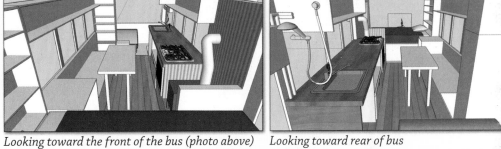

Looking toward rear of bus

"We started our life in the bus
by heading to Baja."

"The best part of the bus is being
able to share it with so many people."

197

A Cabin on Wheels

Matthew Ferrer and Jessi Brooks

Photography by Matthew & Jessi
Interior wide-angle photos by Jon Burton Reesman

"The Flower Ship has allowed us to live in and explore many places; it even evacuated us from a wildfire in 2017!"

Matthew and Jessi are homesteaders, gardeners, herbalists, and visionary artists. Matthew is a woodworker and passionate wood salvager/collector, and dreams of building more tiny homes and mobile spaces.
—LK

IN 2014 WE BOUGHT A 1995 FORD E350 Econoline short bus with a 7.3L Powerstroke diesel engine. We removed all but one of the seats, gave it a psychedelic paint job, a ¾″ plywood floor, basic cabinetry, and a full-size futon. Dubbed "Holy Spirit," we drove her cross-country to California.

In spring 2016, the bus was further transformed. The roof was cut off and a new steel tube frame welded together and bracketed to the original frame. Curved box beam trusses and 2×4s were fastened onto the new steel frame. ⅛-inch plywood was fastened to the framing, creating a curved wooden skin which was fiberglassed and then painted.

The new shell is insulated with recycled wool. The floor and walls are made with cedar fence boards and cabinets are made of too many reclaimed/salvaged woods to name.

There is a small wood stove with a copper heat shield and recycled tile hearth. The stove pipe has a 2-foot section that twist-locks on and off to lower height while driving.

The bed loft has a skylight, two small windows, and a bay window (inspired by our beloved cat). The interior is 6′6″ wide by 15′6″ long, and the height varies from 7′11″ to 8′8″ tall. The exterior height is slightly over 12 feet tall.

It has a small solar system and can run on- or off-grid. All interior lights are LEDs with fader switches. There is an antique copper washtub sink.

It has 10-foot-wide tires and Air Lifts on the rear to stabilize its extra height and weight.

After this conversion, the bus was renamed "The Flower Ship." We've driven her all over the west coast — camping in style at national and state parks, wild hot springs, friend's driveways, turnouts, farms, and festivals.

The Flower Ship has allowed us to live in and explore many places; it even evacuated us from a wildfire in 2017! With the arrival of our son Terran, we sold the bus in 2021 and are currently dreaming of our next road rig!

Matthew: *instagram.com/wood_medicine*
Jessi: *instagram.com/jessiaflower*
Jon Burton: *instagram.com/lostcoastlens*

"The bed loft has a skylight, two small windows, and a bay window (inspired by our beloved cat)."

Towanda

Austin LeMoine & Troy Chebuhar

This is the longest story in the book. It's such complete, useful information that we didn't cut it down.　　　　　　—LK

MEET TOWANDA, OUR 35-FOOT rolling home and workspace. Design and construction was a completely collaborative process and took Troy and me about 18 months. Basically forever, when the road is calling!

Nearly all the materials inside were salvaged/reclaimed, and we estimate the total cost just under $10,000, bus included. We've been living, traveling, and working from the bus for the past four years.

We built the bus to live cheaply. Living in Chicago, we were tired of rent increases, and putting time and effort into improving properties we didn't own. We also wanted to spend more time doing creative work and learning new trades, and less time behind a desk.

These days, our income comes from a variety of sources including carpentry, DJ gigs, music video production, art, and educational workshops. We've crisscrossed the U.S. a number of times over and have found some great jobs on the road, like helping Bob Pittenger with his raccoon problem in Port Townsend, playing records at Fisheye Farms in Detroit, and teaching kids about solar power and small-space design in Albuquerque.

We've hit just about every skatepark along the way (always our first stop in a new town), honed our city stealth-parking skills, and have posted up on more Forest Service roads than we can count. And of course, we've had numerous breakdowns, which are always adventures in their own way.

We certainly weren't carpenters when we started the project, but we'd built a ton of ramps, forts, and tree houses as kids, and we were eager to test our skills building

"We've been living, traveling, and working from the bus for the past four years."

an interior living space from scratch.

Before starting the project, we tried to draw a to-scale layout of the interior but found it impossible to decide on the dimensions of the interior spaces — *e.g.*, how wide should the walkway be? How tall should the counters be? How long should the bench run? We eventually scrapped our drawings and built based on feel, making decisions along the way.

We installed the woodstove first (it was winter, and we needed our adhesives to cure), and then worked clockwise around the bus, ending the build with the media cabinet/record station. This approach resulted in a much more fitting, organic, and aesthetically pleasing space. It was definitely more work this way, but also more fun.

Our main goal throughout the build was to leave the 360-degree windows as unobstructed as possible. Aside from the windshield, every window in the bus is an emergency exit, and can "gullwing" open to allow an awesome cross breeze and open air feeling. We also wanted to avoid a fully straight, hallway-feeling path through the interior, hence the dog leg shape of the front bench.

Sleeping space is minimal; living space is maximized. One bed in back, and one on the front bench, and cleats on walls for hanging hammocks. The front of the bus is the hangout / reading nook / stay-warm-by-the-fire area; the middle of the bus has a kitchen on one side with turntables and records on the opposite side; and the back of the bus is a studio

space, dining table, and shower/bathroom combo.

Although a ton of the interior is built out with wood, there is still a good sprinkling of exposed steel inside, and its ability to hold magnets. (Old hard drive ones are the best!) has been insanely useful for things like hanging curtains, hammocks, artwork, clothes drying, and makeshift window screens.

A large portion of the interior is old white pine, which came from a barn we tore down with a bunch of friends in Wisconson. Other salvaged woods include cypress from a 100-year-old house, deck cedar rescued from a dumpster, oak from Troy's backyard, Craigslist maple for the kitchen, mismatched oak flooring scraps, and a few forgotten redwood and red cedar boards from a garage attic.

All blackened wood was prepared *Shou Sugi Ban (ancient Japanese practice of blackening wood with fire)*. The ceiling is clad with old growth redwood from a decommissioned Chicago water tower, a very generous gift from a friend, ripped from 22"×11"×2.5" boards. Yeah, they were huge. Troy and I jokingly called these boards the "dinosaur bones" because of their age and felt compelled to honor them somehow in the build. These cross sections have an endless amount of grain detail to get lost in: hand-waxed finish to maintain natural color, irregular screw pattern reminiscent of stars in the night sky.

The woodstove was purchased from an ice fisherman in Wisconsin, who also happened to be a Frank Zappa superfan.

It's a small stove, but it's kept us warm for extended ski bum missions in the Rockies. It's also the best coffee and tortilla warmer!

The stove's legs are cut on the back and sit on a platform that hides one of the front wheel wells. The vertical face of the woodstove platform is ash: some steam bent, some soaked in a hot pool clamped to buckets. A garbage-picked classroom U.S. map hangs on cleats next to the woodstove and can be flipped around and used as a projector screen for watching movies.

The overhead shelves were pieced together using pieces of the metal AC ducting we tore out of the original bus interior and other small scraps of redwood and yellow pine. The gray ceiling behind the front bench shelf was removed to increase storage and show the bus's "ribs." The underside has three DC reading lights we made from old wooden bowl sets, which can be turned on or off in any combination.

We spent a lot of time designing the kitchen. We love cooking and knew it was a core component of cheap living, so we really tried to make it a functional space that wouldn't piss us off if we were cooking in it seven days a week. A lot of people have commented that it has more counter space than their apartment, so I think we did okay.

The post supporting the kitchen counter has a wenge *(a type of wood)* top tenon that fits into a countertop mortise. From above, this gives the illusion that the post is a giant piece of exotic wenge —but upon closer inspection of the bark below, it's just white pine. Surprise!

Figuring out how and where to mount the old lab faucet we'd gotten from a high school janitor was a bit difficult. We finally settled on an old fire extinguisher holder screwed to a tiny section of wall between the windows behind the sink. The faucet bolted to the base of the holder where the extinguisher would normally sit, and the latch above holds a lathe-turned cup filled with lighters for the stove.

It was one of those scrappy "aha" moments that turned out really well. Operating the sink involves stepping on the sailboat galley pump recessed in the floor below. It's amazing for conserving

"Our main goal throughout the build was to leave the 360-degree windows as unobstructed as possible."

More...

"A large portion of the interior is old white pine, which came from a barn we tore down."

water. The pump can be feathered to a trickle, or stomped to full flow, and everything in between. And it's hands-free! Clean water comes from a homegrown bucket-based gravity filtration system featuring Berkee filters, which creates potable water from just about any source.

The Sundanzer DC chest freezer is super efficient, reliable, and makes it easy to keep food costs low.

We jazzed it up with cedar and maple to match the interior and framed a large steel sheet in the front for magnets. The underside of the freezer handle is roughly gouged—the unexpected texture is always a surprise for guests! For refrigeration, we rotate frozen reusable ice packs from the freezer into a nearby cooler.

The media cabinet sits directly across from the chest freezer. Underneath the tambour-inspired lid is a wood platter that holds two turntables and a mixer. This platter hangs from four threaded rod posts, one at each corner, held up by four wing nuts that can be adjusted to level the entire turntable platter—important because our parking spots are almost never level, and we do a fair number of DJ gigs outdoors, directly from the bus.

The entire platter can also be dropped and removed from the record cabinet, making it easy to bring our turntables into a venue or bar. The media cabinet is also home to a vintage stereoscope

receiver, cassette deck, and a pullout LP drawer made from recycled toolbox drawer slides.

Records occupy a huge amount of space on the bus. If you look closely, you'll find them stashed everywhere. The shelf above the media cabinet is the bus library, which of course contains a handful of ShelterPub books!

The rear of the bus serves as the studio and workspace. The card catalog drawers between the booth and toilet contain various art supplies, and the work table tilts into a drafting position. The swivel chair in the rear is a Frankenstein creation made with parts from a school cafeteria table and the original bus seat frames. The adjustable shop light was originally used by Troy's grandpa in his workshop, and has since been converted to DC.

The rear shelf holds all clothing, and contains two monitor speakers. The removable "grills" for these speakers were made using parts from the old AC system. These speakers, along with nine ceiling speakers, make up the bus sound system and tie into the receiver and turntables.

The bus bathroom, opposite the table, consists of a simple shower and homegrown composting toilet. The toilet seat rests on a 10-inch blast gate from a dust collection system, its slide closure helps prevent odor and bugs inside the bus. The compost lives outside of the bus

and can be removed and emptied from the exterior.

We made the small shower pan by cutting down a plastic laundry sink. The curtain hangs from an unused bike cable, looped on the ceiling with tiny hooks, and tucks down inside the shower pan to eliminate leaks. The vertical water line to the shower head is hidden inside a wooden post. During cold weather, the shower can be configured to draw water through a hose from a hot pot on the stove instead from the raw water tank below the bus.

All electricity on the bus is supplied by the sun and stored in a six-battery deep-cycle bank below the bus along with our propane and water tanks. The roof sports five 100-watt PV panels mounted on homemade tiltable aluminum racks, installed with the kind help and guidance of the legendary Ed Eaton—a *long-time* solar proponent, activist, builder, teacher, bus dweller, solar cooking specialist, and off-grid liver. Thanks Ed, you rule! And a special shoutout to Kevin, KOB, Karo, Bito, Mejay, Diesel Joe, Musto, Jimmy, Tomahawk, Allie, Zerk, and anyone else I forgot for your help along the way, and of course, our families for their support and encouragement! ***We love ya all!!!***

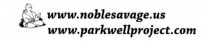
www.noblesavage.us
www.parkwellproject.com

"We've hit just about every skatepark along the way."

"…teaching kids about solar power and small-space design…"

Old Red

Rolf Pot

THE STORY OF THE BUS BEGAN A LONG time ago. I grew up in a small town in the north of The Netherlands in the '50s and '60s. There was a gypsy camp some distance away. I was told to be careful passing by there.

I remember as a kid accelerating on my bicycle when I rode by. I do remember seeing a peaceful setup with beautiful wagons, old cars, and colorful people. That experience made a lasting impression on my young brain.

Soon after getting my driver's license at age 18, I bought an old Citroen 2CV wagon. I immediately got to work, converting it into a tiny rolling home, with the gypsy camp in my mind.

"I took trips mostly along the California coast."

It was a basic rig, with questionable brakes. I cruised everywhere; I was happy as a clam. I was sold on homes on wheels.

I moved to New York in 1977 and settled in Santa Cruz in the spring of '78. I found the bus in 1981. When I saw someone putting a "for sale" sign on it, I was sold! It was in very good, original condition and I was able to buy it for $1,000 — pretty much all I had.

As luck would have it, a lot of loose lumber and other useful materials were lying around and I incorporated those in the conversion process, along with other items I had collected over time.

This rig became my mobile home, and I took trips mostly along the California coast. I ended up living in it for about six years, mostly on 225 forested camp acres where I worked, feeling content and at home.

After moving the bus to a cool backyard at the home of good friends in Santa Cruz, I added a hot tub, made from a large, cut-off garbage can. Hot water (from a small on-demand water heater — brought over from The Netherlands in a suitcase) fed periodically into the top of my precious tub; cool water was released through a valve on the bottom of the tub, down

the front steps of the bus, and into a gravel pit. I have fond memories of squatting in it for long periods of time, meditating and relaxing.

About five years ago, I moved the bus to into its current location at my Santa Cruz home. By that time, it was in serious need of a renovation. I added a small sauna and removed the steering wheel to make room for a flushing toilet.

Old Red could potentially hit the road again, but by my calculations, I'd probably need a cushion on top of the toilet seat in order to drive the bus.

She has maintained her function as guest quarters and occasional personal relaxation and meditation space for my buddy Teresa as well as for me.

The latest and perhaps most interesting function of the bus began when my good friend Yuji and his dog Moo needed a temporary home. Their house and recording studio burned to the ground last year in fires in the Santa Cruz Mountains, where more than 950 homes were destroyed. As a recording artist, Yuji transformed the bus into his own mini-digitalized recording studio. He lived with us here for about six months.

Old Red has become part of the family these past 40 years. I feel blessed that we are growing old together.

*"Old Red has become part of
the family these past 40 years."*

Airstream Conversion

Ryan Hanson

Photos: Dolf Vermeulen Creative

Ryan and Marlin Hanson are brothers who build custom homes on the Sunshine Coast in British Columbia, Canada. One of their timber homes was featured in our book Small Homes (pp. 36–39).

Here are photos and the story of Ryan and his wife, Catherine, transforming a rotting, moldy Airstream into this beautiful interior living space. A silk purse from a sow's ear!

Ryan and Catherine and their two kids lived in the Airstream while they built their house.

–LK

MY WIFE CATHERINE AND I remodeled this Airstream over the course of a winter. We stripped it right down to the frame and built it back up. Here is a brief summary of the process:

- Stripped, gutted, and disposed of rotten/moldy interior

- Came up wth new floor plan together

- Rewired and plumbed for new floor plan. We decided to abandon the 12-volt and holding tank systems and have full hookups so it could be used as a tiny home.

- Covered entire interior in stucco wire and hand-plastered the interior shell to get the compound curves. I did this with my brother-in-law — a lot of work, but we're pleased with the results. It has a nice, natural feel inside.

- Laid salvaged old-growth fir flooring throughout

- Framed interior walls for bathroom, beds, and kitchen cabinetry using fir that we milled, which was left from other projects

- Clad all the interior walls with clear red and yellow cedar rippings left from the mill

- Installed stainless steel counters from local sheet metal place

- Interior painted over plaster by Catherine

- Shower tiled and grouted with black grout by Catherine — a major project with all the curves and tiny tiles!

- Maple slab bathroom vanity and desk built with slabs left from the mill

- Copper bathroom sink was an old bowl found on eBay and drilled out to make a sink. The faucets were in a shed on our property when we bought it; we just had to clean them up and replace the seals.

- Shower glass installed

- Catherine sewed curtains, pillow cases, and bedding with fabric found at thrift stores and Ikea sales.

- Catherine decorated with found and salvaged items.

"Stripped, gutted, and disposed of rotten/moldy interior."

This was a really fun project to do together! We ended up spending very little on materials. The biggest investment was time.

Marlin and I are partners in Hanson Land and Sea and both really appreciate the feedback we've gotten from you over the years!

 www.hansonlandandsea.com
instagram.com/hanson_land_and_sea

"Clad all the interior walls with clear red and yellow cedar rippings left from the mill."

More...

*"Covered entire interior in stucco wire and hand-plastered
the interior shell to get the compound curves."*

"Copper bathroom sink was an old bowl found
on eBay and drilled out to make a sink."

Fran's Bambi
Airstream Design by Chris Deam

The Bambi is the smallest single-axle Airstream trailer and the darling daughter of the family. There's something so appealing about this complete and efficient mini house. It's got a kitchen, bathroom and bedroom — the basics — in a tiny 100-square-foot package. It's cute!

The Bambi is built, like all Airstreams, with aluminum like an airplane fuselage (therefore lightweight), and with an aerodynamic bullet shape.

I recently saw a relatively new Airstream and was surprised at the bright and elegant interior — way different from the older Airstreams that I was familiar with, which had interiors with wooden paneling and cabinets and formica countertops — Cabin Living magazine decor.

Coincidentally, I recently met Chris Deam, a neighbor, through our mutual interests in surfing and mountain bike riding, and it turned out that he was responsible for redesigning Airstream interiors about 20 years ago.

There's a great video of him giving a Ted Talk about the design process in 2002 (at www.cdeam.com/ted-talk), in which he talks about smoothing out the interior so that it reflected the streamlined, modern, high-tech look of the exterior.

Chris is a designer, architect, and formerly creative director of product design for Dwell magazine. Here's his description of his Airstream designs.

—LK

I WAS INITIALLY ATTRACTED TO Airstream trailers because of their vision of modernity, gleaming aluminum skin, aerodynamic shape, and how they embodied the spirit of independence and mobility that has captured the imagination of generations of Americans.

But I also liked that these trailers are not only about individual freedom, but

> *"...their vision of modernity, gleaming aluminum skin, aerodynamic shape, and how they embodied the spirit of independence and mobility..."*

are also about community. And in 1999, I began to notice something interesting: that those same ideals of independence, mobility and community were gaining momentum in the digital/virtual world.

With the advent of the web and wireless technology, suddenly one was free to work anywhere and at any time. What was missing was a modern vehicle to allow this.

I had an idea: why not connect the dots between trailer culture and digital culture? So I began designing a trailer that would enable a new generation of

digital pioneers to work untethered to place and time constraints.

At the time, Airstream interiors were completely disconnected from the modern aerodynamic exterior. It seemed like there had never been a design language developed to express life on the road, and I wanted the interior to deliver on the promise of the exterior.

I began by revealing the aluminum skin on the interior to both bounce more light around and to reflect the colors of the surrounding landscape. I gently curved the wall panels to soften the edges and suggest movement.

I emphasized horizontal lines to make the space feel longer and raised cabinetry off the floor to make it feel as though there is more square footage. I re-conceived the lighting and integrated wireless technology. And lastly, on the exterior, eliminated all super graphics, rubber, and plastic to return the trailer to its most elemental (and durable) state.

These trailers became the International CCD line for Airstream and eventually accounted for half of their overall sales. In the end, these designs ignited a new interest in trailer travel and opened the door to a new era of customization.

 www.cdeam.com/airstream

Windows at eye level bring the outside in, making the space seem bigger.

Edges are round.

Bed in cozy nook

"I gently curved the wall panels to soften the edges and suggest movement."

Seats fold into double bed, so the Bambi can sleep four people.

There's a drain in the floor of the tiny bathroom.

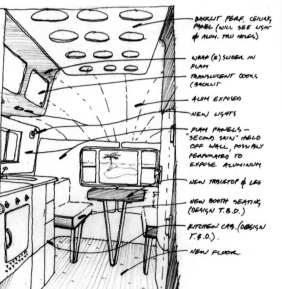

BACKLIT PERF. CEILING PANEL (WILL SEE LIGHT & ALUM. THRU HOLES)

WRAP (S) SLIDER IN PLAM

TRANSLUCENT DOORS (BACKLIT

ALUM EXPOSED

NEW LIGHTS

PLAM PANELS – "SECOND SKIN" HELD OFF WALL, POSSIBLY PERFORATED TO EXPOSE ALUMINUM

NEW TABLETOP & LEG

NEW BOOTH SEATING (DESIGN T.B.D.)

KITCHEN CAB. (DESIGN T.B.D.)

NEW FLOOR.

"I wanted the interior to deliver on the promise of the exterior."

Renovated Lightweight Trailer

Allan Mather

I LIVE ON SALT SPRING ISLAND (IN BRITISH COLUMBIA, CANADA), and last winter, the first one I have spent in the Pacific Northwest in 25 years, with Covid lockdowns and all, I decided I needed a project. So I built what I call my Covid Camper.

I found an old tent trailer — little used, but looking sad — for $500. My objective was to rebuild it as a lightweight trailer.

I am a make-it-up-as-you-go kind of builder, and I was happy to save this old tent trailer from the landfill.

I cranked up the roof, removed the very heavy bed slide-outs and cut off all the canvas. I framed in the walls with spruce 2×2s (ripped 2×4s) and removed the metal riser/roof support posts.

One thing I paid particular attention to was attaching the framing to the trailer base and roof. I used 2×2 top and bottom plates, attached with construction adhesive and many, many self-tapping metal screws.

For the exterior skin, I used 3/16-inch door skin mahogany plywood, insulated with 1½-inch styrofoam, and finished the interior with 5/16-inch pine T&G.

I got some very large used RV windows and reinstalled the original door. For the exterior finish, I used fiberglass mat and many layers of resin, and overlapped the edges on the roof and lower body to ensure it would be weatherproof and hopefully able to withstand the rigors of being towed on rough roads.

Inside, all the cabinetry was removed, except the dinette and the shower base. I built in a single bunk, with coolers, Porta Potti, and the shower base underneath. I found a fold-up foam mattress from Amazon that fit my bunk perfectly. The dinette folds down for a larger bed.

A simple kitchen with a two-burner propane stove, drawers, and a sink was framed in. For the countertop I used a fir slab. The water tank, pump, and 12-volt batteries are under the dinette seats, and a propane water heater was left in its original location, under the stove.

A 100-watt solar panel was attached to the roof, and a vent/fan was put in the roof, over the stove. I have two deep-cycle marine batteries, with a charge controller and a 2,000-watt inverter. I had an old 30-inch TV with a DVD player kicking around, and couldn't resist putting that in, on a swing-out mount. I bought a Little Buddy propane heater, and an attachment so that I can refill one-pound propane bottles from a 20-pounder (such a waste, throwing out those one-pound bottles!). Blackout thermal pull-down curtains were installed, and they work very well.

The walls flare out slightly, and it feels very airy and spacious. I was concerned that the RV windows might be too big, but I am very pleased with all the light they let in.

The trailer tows well behind my Mazda six-cylinder pickup — 90–100 kph easily — but as it is very light, crosswinds can be a bit scary at high speeds!

"I found an old tent trailer — little used, but looking sad — for $500."

"I was happy to save this old tent trailer from the landfill."

"My objective was to rebuild it as a lightweight trailer."

"The walls flare out slightly, and it feels very airy and spacious."

Maisonnettes à Roulettes

Yogan Carpenter

I SPENT A YEAR BUILDING THESE TWO tiny houses for my friends Laure and Alix. We used the same frames, the same materials, and the same dimensions for both.

Editor's note: "Le Chateau Ambulant" is Laure's trailer and is shown on these two pages. "L'Aroubane" is Alix's trailer and is shown on the following two pages.

Their main idea was to be able to move when necessary because, being in their thirties, Alix and Laure weren't sure where they were going to live. After a year, one moved 600km (370 miles), the other 600m (650 yards)!

The idea was to be completely self-sufficient with water, heating, and electricity. Frantz, a good friend, helped us design all the complicated networks of tubes and cables.

Water from the roofs is collected in two 1,000-liter tanks with zinc gutters, then pumped to the water networks with submerged 12-volt pumps powered by photovoltaic electricity. Water is heated with a gas water heater for taking baths —a bit of luxury even in a small space!

The frames are 7.2m (23 feet) × 2.5m (8 feet), but we extended to 8.2m (27 feet) with a tower on one side and a bay windows on the other. So 25m² (270 sq. feet) with the mezzanine!

The frames are made of poplar, a very lightweight wood, like redwood. It has the advantage of being very fibrous, rot-proof, and cheaper than other woods.

The frameworks are insulated with 8cm (3″) of wood wool. The walls are built using 10mm (⅜″) poplar plywood on the outside, (which provides bracing), then covered with 9mm (approximately ⅜″) untrimmed planks of Douglas fir at the bottom, and red cedar shingles at the top. The interiors are sheathed with 5mm (¹⁄₁₆″) ash plywood.

The roofs are covered with Rehpanol, a rubberized roofing membrane that I covered with a vulcanizing copper paint, so the color of the roof changes over time, from pink to brown to a beautiful blue.

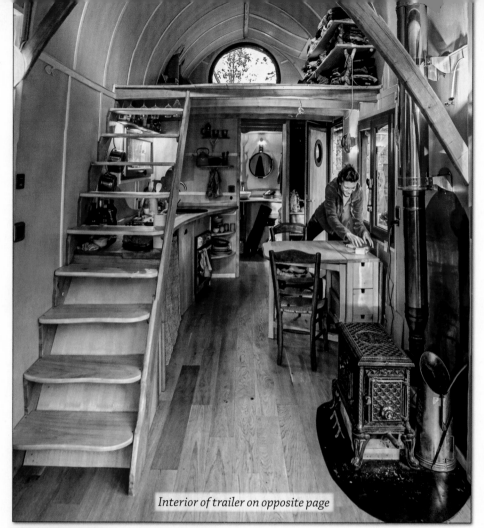

Interior of trailer on opposite page

Left: L'Aroubane; Right: Le Chateau Ambulant

The chimney flashings are copper and the zinc gutters have a stamped aluminum edge to create the curve.

In France we are limited to 3.5 tons for the weight of trailers, which was stressful because it's difficult to calculate the exact weight of buildings like these. We ended up with 3.46 tons for Laure's "Le Chateau Ambulant"and 3.48 tons for Alix's "L'Aroubane" — just under the wire!

Alix moves his house with a 140 hp Iveco tractor.

I will not do another project like this; it's too difficult to keep them lightweight!

www.copeauxcabana.fr
yogan.over-blog.com
instagram.com/yogancarpenter

L'Aroubane

"The idea was to be completely self-sufficient with water, heating, and electricity."

More . . .

Le Chateau Ambulant

Leo, Isao, Madelaine, Lucile, Marti, Rod, Benoix,
Tom, Emily, Brunelle, Yogan

"Their main idea was to be able to move when necessary."

Wandering Star II
Monique Sady

"I wanted to camp in it at Burning Man."

More…

HELLO LLOYD, FIRST LET ME SAY THAT I AM THE PROUD OWNER OF *Home Work*! And I have enjoyed following you on Instagram as well!

I lent *Home Work* to my mom about 12 years ago or so and she was inspired by the "On the Road" section and the gypsy wagons.

She wanted to turn one of my parents' huge metal water tanks into a gypsy cart guest room on their property in the Santa Cruz Mountains. She began collecting crazy quilts and all sorts of things she wanted to decorate it with. Sadly, she passed away in 2012 and never created her gypsy wagon.

She inspired me to do this project, so I started looking for horse trailers in early 2019. As the end of July rolled around, the key for me was to find one in relatively good condition that was also airtight, since I wanted to camp in it at Burning Man, where dust storms are notorious for getting into everything.

I found this 1976 Haynes horse trailer on Craigslist and had only a month to fix it up and decorate it for its maiden voyage out to Black Rock City.

My dad welded the frame for the bed, fixed the floorboards, and made me a little ladder to get up to the bunk. My husband rewired the brake lights (for my safe travels).

I cut and stained some patterned wood trim that covered the old aluminum window frames. (The windows themselves are the original material and have an aqua color to them.)

I decorated the inside with some family heirloom items, like my mom's wood guitar, old family photos of my great-great-grandfather, and my great-grandmother's postcards from the early 1900s that her father, a world-traveling merchant from San Francisco, sent to her from around the world.

I got a few other Boho-themed items from my dad's house. (He is a lifelong, thrift shop bargain hunter, so I can find almost anything I can think of at his house!)

"*I found this 1976 Haynes horse trailer on Craigslist.*"

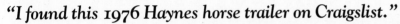

"I felt that by making this horse trailer come to life with my family heirlooms, I'd be honoring that part of my family history."

Wandering Star ll is named after my 98-year-old grandfather's sailboat, which he built up from the base of a fiberglass hull as I was growing up. I felt that by making this horse trailer come to life with my family heirlooms, I'd be honoring that part of my family history as well.

He named the boat Wandering Star, based on the song from the old musical *Paint Your Wagon*, where Lee Marvin sings, "I was born under a wandering star...." I feel like the little horse trailer has that same spirit of adventure when we bring her out to the remote Nevada desert!

I love keeping the back doors wide open in nice weather, and I love the full-size "Haynes Walk-Thru" door in front, which most small horse trailers do not have — they only have half doors that open for hay storage.

I left some parts of the trailer undecorated because I love the interior as is, including the bumper pads and the beautiful, original wood panelling.

And lastly, a bit about myself: I am a wedding photojournalist, with a background as a newspaper photographer. I would call myself an eclectic artist; I make jewelry and costumes, and have discovered baking sourdough bread this past year thanks to the pandemic!

My husband and I work out of our home, so we take a lot of road trips! During 2020, because of Covid we focused on remote areas of Nevada, where we slept in the back of our Tacoma pickup truck on BLM land.

I would say that my little Boho horse trailer wagon is mainly for Burning Man and a few fun-themed trips, like one we'll be taking for my 50th birthday this year!

 www.photographybymonique.com/blog
www.tahoeweddingphotojournalism.com

The Wonder Wagon
Stevie Hudson and Margarita Prokofyeva

BUILDING IS THE DIRECT PRACTICE OF actualizing dreams. We are always dreaming up fun things to create — a universal talent we all hold — but bringing those dreams to life is another story.

I was drawn to building because of the practicality and utility of knowing how to create shelter, but what kept me going was realizing that we can make these necessary nests endlessly beautiful and nourishing for the soul.

With the Wonder Wagon, we wanted to make sure we were learning and challenging ourselves creatively, honing our craft, and creating art. By living in the previous tiny house we built for a year, we had a better understanding of what we liked, what worked, and what didn't.

We decided on a loft and a dual-level curved roof, which would be both beautiful and challenging. It's important for us to be in tune with nature when we build, so we are always using high-quality materials.

We exposed the curved rafters we made with local poplar and finished them with hemp oil. We handcrafted a copper standing seam roof with the help of our friends from The Highland Farm. We decorated the home with cedar shakes and adorned the interior with handmade everything, using a variety of local materials once again.

It's like a museum of Virginia woods; whereever you look, you'll see tulip poplar, Eastern red cedar, cherry, walnut, yellow pine, red and white oak, and even 10-year-old reclaimed Virginia heart pine, most of which is from our friend's farm.

We insulated the house with Havelock sheep's wool and used leftovers to make lamp shades and fill the couch cushions. We made a truth window night light in the loft so you can see the sheep's wool that insulates the house at all times.

We take pride in our work, including the guts! We even got custom handles made for the drawers and closet by our friend at Map Glass.

When you build a home like this, it tells a story. It breathes. When you walk in, you feel like you are in something still living life to the fullest. It's as if the trees are hugging you.

The space itself calms the mind like a deep breath of fresh air. The feeling in these tiny temples is what makes us excited to continue our building journeys and to keep finding fun ways to share these creations with the world. Follow your intuition and believe in your dreams. If you believe in yourself, you really can do anything you set your mind to!

 instagram.com/wonderrigs

See Stevie and Margarita's other project, the Lotus Pod, on pp. 116–117.

"Building is the direct practice of actualizing dreams."

More...

"The space itself calms the mind like a deep breath of fresh air."

Philippa's Folding Cabin on Wheels

Philippa Battye   **Photos by Chris Goodman**

"A key aspect of the design was to have elements which are demountable and could be removed for transit."

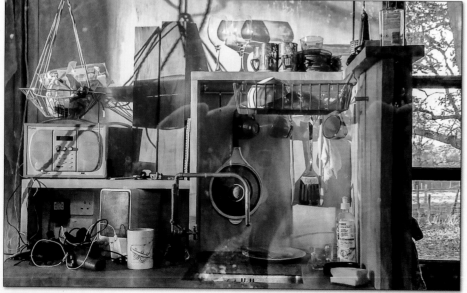

For the past few years, I spent as much free time as I could riding my bicycle, carrying everything I needed to sleep, eat, and stay dry and warm. This was when I felt most content and free.

I realized that to sustain this freedom to roam, I couldn't be harnessed by a mortgage or owned by a bank—forced to do work which wasn't fulfilling in order to sustain a lifestyle I didn't need.

I wanted to meander through life, not hurry through a life less lived—so I decided to build a cabin on wheels.

The idea was cooked up with Stephen West—a neighbor, friend, and critically, a skilled builder. We began the project together, bringing our respective skills (I'm an architect) to the table, working collaboratively to get the build started.

With our combined skills, we felt we could challenge the constraints of a road-towable home. A key aspect of the design was to have elements which are demountable and could be removed for transit.

The two "wings" cantilever off the trailer chassis, hanging from the ash frame with split battens and just a couple of selectively-placed bolts.

The roof structure consists of CNC'd* plywood rafters which slot into a plywood "shelf," each pair of rafters braced at three points with copper poles threaded between them, book-ended by hanging gables.

The roof is then covered in two giant blankets of sheep's wool and a canvas cover. The elements which move are clad in cedar shingles for lightness, the fixed walls in vertical charred larch boards.

In its compact state, the cabana van measures 2.5m wide by 3.6m high (8′ × 11′10″); once expanded: 4.1m at its maximum width by 5.5m high (13′5″ × 18′½″). (Maximum width for a trailer in the U.S.A. is 8 feet.)

We used as much reclaimed material as possible, all doors and windows scavenged from within walking distance of the site. The weathered oak boards used for the parquet floor and sleeping platform lived a former life cladding a house in the

CNC: Computer Numerical Control, a computerized machining process for "removing material from a stock piece."

nearby woods. The structural frame is ash, felled in the woods adjacent to where it was built.

The lightweight tent-like structure, which forms much of the exterior, connects me closely to the natural world around me, making me feel content to be in the elements rather than in an environment created to shut them out.

As the wind whips around and under the canvas, the cabin swings lightly like a boat, and the mornings are delightfully bracing until the wood burner roars, kicking out heat.

I hope that life in a movable shelter — where the orientation, light, and views can change — can assimilate a touch of what I experienced when traveling by bike. Tapping into our nomadic ancestry, waking in new places with renewed perspectives full of wonder and what-ifs — that's what freedom means to me.

Life is fleeting, filled with uncertainty and untrammeled possibilities ready to be tapped into — this is where I hope to spend more of my time.

 *www.philippabattye.com*

> *"I realized that to sustain this freedom to roam I couldn't be harnessed by a mortgage or owned by a bank."*

> *"Life is fleeting, filled with uncertainty and untrammeled possibility waiting to be tapped into."*

Caraban: The Trailblazer
David Bouldy

"We decided to build a small, lightweight trailer made of wood."

AT FIRST, WE HAD JUST A CAMPER VAN, a 2002 Volkswagen Transporter T4 EuroVan (long wheelbase, front engine, 102hp)—great to drive almost anywhere. Then we had a second child, so we needed to find a solution for our travels—we wanted a bit more space to live comfortably.

We thought about it for a while, and instead of changing our camper van, we decided to build a small, lightweight trailer made of wood.

The project began with a sketch and then a computer-assisted design to calculate the weight, since we wanted to make it as light as possible and be really mobile.

We bought a 4m × 2m (13′ × 6.5′) caravan chassis in France with all its paperwork in order. What's more, the chassis was in great shape even though it was built in 1987. The name on the paperwork was *La Bohème* (the bohemian)—a good omen since we wanted to make a gypsy caravan!

The first step was to insulate the bottom with extruded polyurethane, which isn't particularly ecological but is waterproof, and then 3-ply spruce plywood, and the floor was ready.

The rest of the trailer was made of poplar, a very lightweight wood like red cedar.

We cut curved pieces from large planks for the framing, then covered the frame with 5mm (0.2″) plywood, 20mm (0.78″) expanded cork, and then another 0.2″ layer of plywood, then glued and screwed it together like a sandwich.

We put EPDM rubber on the roof and painted the walls. The windows are made of polycarbonate, which is light and solid.

Inside, we've got all the mod-cons of a small cabin: sink, gas stove, a bed/table, and soon, a wood stove and shower!

The trailer weighs 1000kg (2200 lbs). We'd have preferred it to weigh a little less (750kg) so that we wouldn't have

Caraban at right, Yogan's "Le Benne Benz" (see pp. 168–173) at left on a trip the two families took to Portugal together

needed a special driver's license, but that didn't work out.

It's easy to tow, and a few weeks after finishing it, we set off with our two children and the Yogan family, traveling over 3,000 miles and touring Portugal!

Thank you for all you do, for the books, for the dreams — we are children of Shelter Publications!

**yogan.over-blog.com
www.cabanophiles.com**

"We set off with our two children and the Yogan family, traveling over 3,000 miles and touring Portugal!"

More...

"Inside, we've got all the mod-cons of a small cabin."

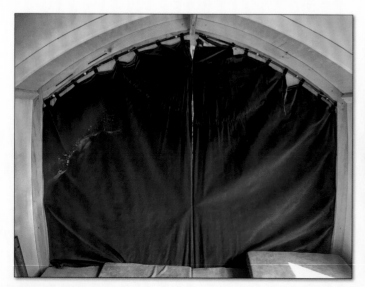

"We are children of Shelter Publications!"

Moksha's Handmade Lightweight Trailers
Moksha Osgood

I was driving home from Pt. Arena along the coast one day and saw this unique trailer parked at Salmon Creek Beach. I stopped and met Mira Nussbaum, an artist who had taken her trailer to the beach and was working on her hand-painted scarves while enjoying the ocean view.

She said the trailer was very lightweight, and in fact, she had towed it there with her Honda CR-V.

It turned out it was built by Moksha Osgood, a woodworker who has created a series of lightweight trailers and small dwellings.

On this page are my photos of Mira and her trailer. On the opposite page are photos by Moksha of this model and two other models, along with vital statistics of each.

Here is Moksha's brief description of his work.

—LK

I AM A PRACTICAL ARTIST WHO ENJOYS imagining and creating innovative dwellings tucked into forest landscapes. I spent the first 15 years of my career building cabinetry and furniture, and eight years ago, I transitioned into building small dwellings.

I have lived in a variety of tiny homes over the last 15 years and this has informed the choices that I make in my designs. My design goals are a mix of sustainability, affordability, and beauty.

I live in Lake County, California, where I have a wood shop and laboratory which are the home of my creations. I use salvaged logs and lumber that I source locally; I choose sustainable materials like sheep's wool or mineral wool for insulation; and I integrate off-grid solar for the energy needs of the dwellings that I build.

I am passionate about helping to provide people with low-overhead housing solutions because of how my own affordable small dwellings have freed up time and resources to pursue the things that I deeply care about.

Beauty helps us stay awake to the sensory world, to directly experience the specific forms of value that living in this world can provide for us.

—Moksha

 Moksha: ***www.mokshadesigns.net***
Mira: ***www.silkstorymaps.com***

Mira uses the trailer as an oceanside studio to meet with clients for her art business, Silk Stories, where she paints people's stories of transformation on silk tapestries.

WINDOW SEAT The exterior is a combination of marine grade plywood, redwood doors and windows, bent laminations, and 24-gauge galvanized sheet metal for the arched surfaces. Insulation is 2″ R-13 polyiso rigid foam insulation. The interior wall paneling is custom-milled redwood, the seating and transformer bed is Douglas fir, and the slide-out drawers below the seats are maple plywood. There is storage behind each of the seat backs, and RGB LED cove lighting that runs around the perimeter of the ceiling. This model starts at $21,000.

"Beauty helps us stay awake to the sensory world."

ABIDE This model includes a two-burner stove, a small sink, 6 LED light sconces, and a bench seat that folds out into a full-size bed. It has fully insulated walls and roof, double-pane windows, a birch plywood interior, a Meranti marine-grade plywood exterior, and removable arch canopies for easy road travel. It is 50 sq. ft., weighs 1500 lbs., and is comfortable for one or two people. This model starts at $24,000.

"My design goals are a mix of sustainability, affordability, and beauty."

INCUBATE This model has a two-burner Atwood cook stove, a sink with a gravity-fed faucet, four LED light sconces, a large solid maple kitchen counter, and maple sliding cabinet doors. There is a full-size bed with two drawers underneath and Douglas fir plywood interior paneling. The exterior is a mix of salvaged and new redwood and cedar siding; 26-gauge galvanized sheet metal covers the arch roof and sides. There are two Douglas fir French doors, a 3′×4′ PVC sliding double-pane window, redwood steps, a redwood bent-lamination canopy frame (can be disassembled for road travel), and an 18 oz. PVC canvas canopy. It is built on a 12′ Carson utility trailer and weighs 2,700 lbs. The starting price for this model is $29,000.

"I use salvaged logs and lumber that I source locally."

"When people ask how we manage to live in such a tiny space with two kids,
we answer happily that we've never felt so comfortable in a home!"

Tiny Home in France for Family of Four

Tomas & Stephanie Strac

Hi, Lloyd,

Here are some photos of our tiny house that we just finished building for our family of four, out here in the countryside of central France.

My partner and I started the design process last summer (just before we found out she was pregnant), started construction in October, and moved in in February, just in time for our baby to be born in the "living room!"

We spent a lot of time working on a design that would be both functional and comfortable, allowing us to meet the needs of our daily life while maintaining enough open space to move around and play without stepping on each other.

We achieved this by pushing the kitchen and bathroom to either end of the main level, keeping the rest of the space relatively open, aside from our built-in couch and bench, which cover the wheel wells.

High ceilings, large windows, light colors, and lots of natural light complement this design, leaving our main living space feeling light, open, and spacious despite its small size.

When we say small, however, we should mention that this house is quite large compared to other tiny houses, at least in France. Since we were designing a space to live in for at least a few years with two small but growing children, we were rather ambitious and really pushed the limits of what is possible sizewise.

The house's large size meant we had to be really careful about the materials we used, so as not to exceed the 3½-ton weight limit (for trailers of that category) in France. For this reason, we used lightweight, thin poplar for the floors and wall coverings, and most of the interior furniture, as well as the exterior siding, is removable to minimize weight during transport. In other words, our house isn't meant to be moved too frequently.

Our home has two loft spaces —one bedroom for us, and the other a bedroom and play space for our kids. Our three-year-old, Maya, can still stand up in her loft, and we imagine she will be able to for another couple of years.

Our bathroom is quite spacious as well because of a few rather luxurious elements that make life easier with kids. The first of these is the inclusion of a bathtub instead of a shower, because it is much more practical for small children, despite taking a bit more space.

At the last moment we added a washing machine, because we use washable diapers for our baby and neither of us was keen on spending our days washing them by hand.

The house was built using only repurposed and/or eco-friendly materials; thanks to its efficient insulation and passive-solar design, we hardly burned any wood this winter to keep ourselves warm, even with a newborn.

We built it on a trailer, custom built for tiny homes, that measures 28 × 8 feet. The curving slopes on the front and back of the house add about an extra meter to each loft without compromising ceiling height in the living area, and allow for extra hidden storage space in the kitchen and bathroom. This makes the house 30m² total (345 sq. ft.), including the two lofts.

We wanted to find a balance between efficient design and creative shapes and unexpected details to keep the overall aesthetic beautiful and light on the eyes. Some examples are the use of round windows, copper tubes as curtain rods, and the use of curves to blend the re-used wood and galvanized metal that we salvaged from old, nearby buildings for the exterior siding.

When people ask how we manage living in such a tiny space with two kids, we answer happily that we've never felt so comfortable in a home!

Efficient use of space, good organization, and a simple lifestyle that keeps material possessions to a minimum leaves us feeling light and free in our daily lives.

The housework is done in 10 minutes, the cost of living is reduced, and we have more time and energy to spend together as a family.

We've found that the natural light, warmth, and views of the beautiful nature surrounding us have had a positive effect on our inner wellbeing, especially after having spent years living in the dark, cold, traditional stone houses of our region. We have also decreased our energy consumption—we almost never turn on lights in the summertime, and use them much less often in winter.

Your books and all of the great ideas in them were a big inspiration for this house and other projects in my work as a carpenter and builder. Thanks for all of your work!

Amicalement,
Tomas and Stephanie

> **"High ceilings, large windows, light colors, and lots of natural light complement this design."**

> **"This house is quite large compared to other tiny houses, at least in France."**

Vardo in Connecticut

Jack Collins

SO DID IT START AS A BET OR A DARE? I'm not sure. I'd been talking about building a vardo for so long that when a stripped-down old camp trailer frame suddenly showed up in my yard, I knew I had to get to work.

Thanks, neighbor Justin, for the shove!

I'd been a builder and cabinet maker, with a specialty lumber business for 30 years. Recently retired and with all this nice wood still needing a final home, the time was right.

We wanted something simple and light that we could move around the farm, and set up with a new view, seasonally.

Jane and I built our passive solar home 40 years ago on this former tired-out Connecticut dairy farm. We have been growing and putting up a year's worth of food every year since, so we don't get much opportunity to travel. We were looking to create something in which to camp, meditate, bird watch, wood carve, play music, and write a few songs.

I used to work with a really creative carpenter buddy. In the '70s we tore down old tobacco sheds and built restaurants and nightclubs with the recycled wood. He always wanted to build greenhouses with laminated bent rafters. He passed away in the '90s before we ever got to do one. In his memory, I wanted to explore that idea, so this became kind of a prototype/practice project for bending some ash.

Northeastern Connecticut has been hit hard by the Asian ash borer and I wanted to save a bit from the farm before it was all gone. Ash being a good bending wood, I had Justin saw 150 ⅜-inch-thick × 2½-inch × 12-foot-long slats, air-dried them for a few months, and, after making the jig, put them together with three gallons of Titebond glue and every clamp I owned or could borrow.

There are at least 14 species of wood used in this project: including pitch pine for framing, ash, sassafras, 100+-year-old chestnut, white pine, larch, three kinds of cedar, walnut, and butternut.

I hand-split the shakes from recycled Western red cedar high-tension power poles. The power company has been replacing them with metal poles. The wooden ones have been in use for years all around New England. Virgin growth stuff, just beautiful, and they don't grow around here.

I sprung for the standing seam roof when I couldn't find wide enough one-piece rubber as originally planned. Pricey but lasts forever.

It took about a year and a half of putzing around to get it 90% completed. I still have all the little homey things to finish up. And then maybe get going on that greenhouse.

VITAL STATISTICS

- Renogy 100W solar panel powers a deep-cell 12V system for lights, fan, and charging devices. Also wired for 110V for a generator
- Cubic Grizzly woodstove with oven
- 5-gal. jugs for water to sink
- Composting sawdust toilet with access to an outside trap door for clean-out

"There are at least 14 species of wood used in this project."

"*We wanted something simple and light that we could move around the farm.*"

Modern Vardo
Greg Ryan and Jill Baron

Wagon inspires impromptu jam session on its maiden voyage.

"Traveling with it was like pulling a cartload of puppies behind us."

Living on the road: a life-changing experience, disorienting and unsettling at first. It wasn't easy leaving the comforts of home and our settled routines, much less adjusting to living in a space smaller than our bathroom. Cold showers, shabby laundromats, never having enough fresh vegetables.

A roller coaster of exhilarating ups and discouraging downs. Living on the road, as with any adventure, tests your mettle. Sometimes we didn't know when or where we'd end up for the night, if we'd have to set up in the dark, or if we'd be safe.

Living in a handmade, rolling home requires hands-on skills. Neither of us is handy or mechanically inclined, and we found ourselves in situations we didn't think we could handle. But digging deep, we found resourcefulness we didn't know we had.

The wagon was a joy to be in, and traveling with it was like pulling a cartload of puppies behind us. Wherever we stopped, people came running, pressing their faces to the windows. More than once, finding ourselves with no place to stay for the night, we were invited to dinner and to spend the night in the driveway of an appreciative stranger. The wagon was our talisman of goodwill.

On the road, life does become simpler, if no less challenging. Wearing the same clothes day after day, washing hair with cold water from a hose, managing with less of everything. Forgoing dinner to watch the sky turn pink, perched on top of the picnic table with a bag of chips. On the road, you become a bit feral, your intuition keener. More in the moment, less in your own head. With no schedules and no set plans, more spontaneous and receptive.

The wagon was our magic red carpet, a portal to experience not available to us otherwise. A trek through the desert with a medicine man. An invitation to a Mardi Gras potluck in a tiny village of French heritage, Cajun music blaring from portable radios. Improvisational potlucks and hours by the fire with fellow wanderers we had just met. Everyone with a story. Outdoors, under the stars, everyone open to the magic.

We'll never see most of those people again. But on the road, connections can feel more authentic, more powerful, and remarkably close, even after only a few hours. Our dearest friends include people we met on the road, and those relationships led us to adventures we could not have imagined, including an African camping safari and even a new home in New Mexico. All paths leading back to our gypsy wagon travels.

Changing our lives, changing us.

—Jill Baron

"On the road, life does become simpler, if no less challenging."

VITAL STATISTICS

- **Floor area:** 84 sq. ft.
- Solar panels charge 12V DC 100Ah agm battery, which runs 2 DC fans.
- Small inverter runs AC loads.
- **Heat:** Suburban 15,000 btu propane heater (turned out to be too big for the space, better choice would have been small Dickinson Marine Cozy Cabin marine heater).
- Hot and cold running water
- Fresh and greywater storage tanks
- Self-contained portable toilet
- Propane refrigerator
- Two-burner propane cook stove

"The wagon was our magic red carpet."

Surfers' Transcontinental Road Trip in Tuk-Tuk

Story by Sam George in *The Surfer's Journal*

Photos by Luke Alcorn and Leo Hetzl

THROUGHOUT MY 40-PLUS YEARS OF international service travel and exploration, I've encountered plenty of eccentric "road-less-traveled" devotees on the barefoot pilgrim's trail. But only very occasionally do you meet those who have taken their offbeat surfaris to such extreme lengths that even the most seasoned surf adventurers shake their heads.

Meet Luke Alcorn and Fumi Ishizaki, two surfers who completed an extraordinary road trip in May 2020: driving from Mexico City to Patagonia in a tuk-tuk. Yes, a tuk-tuk: one of those tiny, motorized rickshaws found putt-putting through congested roundabouts in exotic cities like Bangkok, Colombo, or Mumbai, serving—so long as no steep hills are in sight—as single passenger taxis or grocery delivery carts.

Three wheels. Small cabin. Handlebar controls. A single driver's seat and passenger storage space in the rear. As vehicles, they are almost ridiculous. The average golf cart is more formidable. Tuk-tuks are in no way intended or suitable for a perilous, transcontinental road trip through Central and South America.

But in the summer of 2017, that was exactly what Alcorn and Ishizaki set out to accomplish, Their tiny tuk-tuk loaded down with two adults, a meager array of worldly goods, five surfboards, and no toilet. With Alcorn at the handlebars and Ishizaki perched on a makeshift seat behind, the pair made their way down the coast of mainland Mexico, through the mountains of Guatemala, nicking the corner of Honduras, and back to the sea in El Salvador while skirting Lake Nicaragua.

They spent the summer of 2019 broken down on Costa Rica's fabled Osa Peninsula before rolling into Panama. From there, they flew the tuk-tuk to Bogotá, Colombia (with less hassle than shipping their boards), loaded back up, and proceeded down the coast, sailing

"I have never met a simpler, more authentic, more pure pair of travelers."

through their umpteenth border, crossing into Ecuador and along its coast, on to Peru and up into the Andes, then back to the coast and Chicama.

Then to Lima and Miraflores, before pushing their way into Chile, climbing east over the mountains into Argentina. They stayed along the coast before crossing back over the tip of the continent into Patagonia. There, they finally coasted to a halt, having successfully navigated all the miles and jungles and rivers and mountains, with challenges innumerable, across an entire continent.

These sorts of remarkable stories can, in fact, be heard wherever surf sojourners gather in the far-flung corners of the world —Padang's old Batang Arau hotel, the campground at Lafitenia, Restaurante Punta Roca in La Libertad. At these and many other stops on *The Endless Summer*'s devotional trail, one is bound to encounter plenty of hardcore travelers.

But I can say this: I have never met a simpler, more authentic, more *pure* pair of travelers. Judged not merely by the chosen mode of travel, but by what this humble little tuk-tuk represents: the *how* of their travels. No pretense. No expectations. Able to laugh at the absurdity of their intentions, yet resolutely moving forward, albeit on the highway shoulder.

"...having successfully navigated all the miles and jungles and rivers and mountains, with challenges innumerable, across an entire continent."

Torres del Paine National Park, Patagonia

Confronting myriad trials and joys with equanimity fostered at the handlebars of an older, loaded trike whose top speed rarely exceeded 20 mph. Smiling at the unfamiliar miles scrolling slowly under their three wheels, confident that these new worlds encountered will smile back for no reason other than because the sight of two surfers — one from Australia, the other from Japan — scaling mountains, fording rivers, and traversing continents in a tuk-tuk is just about the craziest thing anyone has ever seen.

So what did Alcorn and Ishizaki do when they reached their destination? They simply fired up the tuk-tuk and, in a pandemic-beating rush (at 20 mph, remember), crossed back across the Patagonian *cordillera* into Argentina, pointed north up the continent's east coast with the prevailing southwest wind at their backs, then went back to Santiago with borders snapping shut behind them the whole way. After finding a kind Chilean family who happily agreed to store the tuk-tuk, they caught a flight out of Arturo Marino Benitez airport and winged their way home to Sydney.

More...

Pit stop with a condor in Nazca, Peru

Hanging in Costa Rica

"The pair made their way down the coast of mainland Mexico, through
the mountains of Guatemala, nicking the corner of Honduras,
and back to the sea in El Salvador while skirting Lake Nicaragua."

$1 a night for this cozy little beach shack in Nicaragua

A minor hiccup on the Osa Peninsula,
Costa Rica

Endless waves in El Salvador

"Confronting myriad trials and joys with equanimity fostered at the
handlebars of an older, loaded trike whose top speed rarely exceeded 20 mph."

Sunrise on the Osa Peninsula in Costa Rica

Antofagasta, northern Chile

More...

Beach shack somewhere in the Peruvian desert

Roadside stop somewhere in Chile

At 4,700 meters above sea level in the Peruvian Andes

En route to El Chaltén, a small mountain village in the Patagonia region of southern Argentina, near the border with Chile

Epilog: After leaving the tuk-tuk in Chile, Luke and Fumi bought a 1986 28-foot Compass yacht built in Australia and are sailing the high seas, with the intent of eventually sailing to Chile and resuming their tuk-tuk adventures. Luke recently wrote that if all goes as planned, they will sail to Chile, and "...be reunited with Octavio, our trusty tuk-tuk, and finish our adventure back up through Chile, Argentina, Bolivia, Peru — then continue back through Central America to Mexico, and after that, fly back to Panama and sail across the Pacific Ocean to Australia. It's a big dream, but a dream worth making come true."

"It's a big dream, but a dream worth making come true."

The Winnebiko

A 10,000-Mile, Computerized Bicycle Trip Through America in the '80s

Steven K. Roberts

*Steve Roberts is a prolific designer — recumbent bikes, boats, a mobile lab, and a number of other unique inventions — all detailed extensively on his website, **www.microship.com**.*

On these two pages, we're covering his first recumbent bike, the Winnebiko, built in the '80s. It's the simplest of his bikes, and the easiest to understand, especially compared to his 1989–91 BEHEMOTH (Big Electronic Human-Energized Machine — Only Too Heavy), a 580-pound, 105-speed monster, costing some $1.2 million(!), a 3-year project supported by Sun Microsystems and about 140 other corporate sponsors. (BEHEMOTH is now ensconced in the Computer History Museum in Mountain View, California.)

Steve has posted an awesome amount of details on all his creations, so you can delve as deep as you wish with any of them, but this earlier model is a lot easier for mere mortals to understand, and therefore presented here.

Steve is not only a brilliant inventor, but a good writer; I really enjoyed reading his book on the Winnebiko, Computing Across America: The Bicycle Odyssey of a High-Tech Nomad *(available via* **microship.com***). It's full of great adventures ("joy and despair") and interesting details of his 10,000-mile zig-zag trip across the U.S.A.*

Photo by Katy Peden

Here is Steve's description of the trip, along with a few quotes from his book. On the next two pages are brief accounts of his other two bikes. —LK

P.S.: Check out the beautiful trimaran he's since designed and built, the "Microship: An Amphibian Pedal/Solar/Sail Micro-Trimaran" on his website.

Rolling into Huntsville, Texas, May, 1984. Photo by Jimmie Morris

All photos by Steve except those noted

"What's the matter, Steve? You going to be a bum all your life?"
–Steve's mom upon learning of his plans to sell his house in Ohio and move to a bicycle

THIS TECHNOMADIC STORY BEGINS at a time of primitive computer and communications technologies. Cellular phones did not yet exist, online services cost a few dollars an hour for cumbersome text-only services, and people were debating whether one could actually work at home instead of the office.

I had just turned 30, and was on a quest for geek adventure fueled by publishing — a way to escape Ohio suburbia and combine all my passions into a nomadic lifestyle. After six months of obsessive preparation, I hit the road in September, 1983 on a custom recumbent bicycle with a solar-powered portable computer (the venerable Radio Shack Model 100), a CompuServe account, and a base office.

The idea was to simply have a way to stay in touch with clients and publishers while traveling full time, and as the months passed, I refined the toolset to render my physical location less and less relevant. "Work at home? Work anywhere!," I wrote exuberantly, sensing that I was pedaling at the cusp of major cultural change.

This started simply as a high-tech bicycle tour, but what I didn't expect was that the media would be enchanted by the idea of nomadic connectivity — combining new information tools into a mobile lifestyle that also happened to be visually distinctive with the recumbent bicycle, solar panels, antennas, and more. My bike trip was becoming a career.

As the adventure unfolded, I wrote a book called *Computing Across America*, produced columns and features for various magazines, did interviews, and watched my whole life change. Ohio suburbia faded to a speck in my rear-view mirror, and I began fantasizing about the next generation of technomadic tools.

This first trip took place between 1983 and 1985, but the technological world was rapidly evolving and parts quickly came to feel obsolete. By late 1984, I had switched to a much more capable Hewlett Packard Portable, and was designing a system to let me type on a handlebar keyboard while riding, as well as maintaining a steady wireless link to readers. When the 10,000-mile mark rolled around (appropriately enough, in Silicon Valley), I decided to take a year off from the road to finish the book and build a whole new system onto the trusty frame that had carried me thus far.

High tech camping, 1984. Photo by Katy Peden

Crossing Dallas Divide in Colorado, en route to Telluride. (September, 1984)

*Daily routine was to use payphone to check mail and forums.
Photo by Dan Burden*

VITAL STATISTICS, WINNEBIKO (1983–84)

Fabricated over a 6-month period leading up to initial departure on September 28, 1983, this was the elemental form of my technomadic adventure substrate. The overall weight including packs varied during the 10,000-mile tour from 135 to 195 pounds, and gearing was a straightforward wide-range 18-speed system.

Basic Mechanical Features

- 48-spoke, 27″ undished rear wheel
- 16″ front wheel
- Under-seat steering with stainless steel tie-rod to fork
- Blackburn rack carrying initial standard touring load, gradually refined during trip
- 4130 Chrome-Moly frame, lugless, filleted/brazed construction, triple stays, built by Franklin Frames (Jack Trumbull)
- Small zipper fairing around handlebar pack for electronics, mounted in front of head tube
- Crossover drive with 1:1 input chain and 18-speed derailleur, forward bottom bracket in tandem-style eccentric

Electronics

- Simple electronics package mounted above front wheel; under-seat switch box
- "Push" speed/distance sensor, later the Cat-Eye Solar
- Paging security system with piezoelectric vibration sensor
- CB radio for emergencies
- 12V battery for lights and other loads, 5W solar panel, and AC charger
- Yellow barricade flasher behind seat, xenon strobe on pole, taillight, sealed-beam headlight
- Radio Shack Model 100 laptop in pack; later the HP-110 portable

"The task was easy enough to define: all I had to do was dismantle an active lifestyle, create a high-tech bicycle, install my home and office on the stern, and then pedal the whole affair around the United States while continuing to write for a living…. No problem."

More...

Winnebiko II

10,000 miles on the first version gave me lots of time to fantasize about what I really wanted: a binary chord keyboard in the handlebars talking to a computer screen on the console. In the summer of 1986, I built the Winnebiko II system onto the same recumbent frame, with a computer that let me type in binary at about 35 words-per-minute while riding. There was also a packet-radio mailbox for email and chatting with fellow hams, and the bike was equipped with a speech synthesizer to let me remotely chat with people standing around the bike.

The version covered an additional 6,000 miles on both coasts of the U.S. The network culture was also growing rapidly, becoming quite a community—an online sense of home that by now had completely replaced the geographic one I long ago left behind in Ohio.

But technology was also exploding, and by 1988 I was again having serious geek fantasies. I paused on the second trip in Florida when my *Computing Across America* book came out, and after few months on the speaking circuit (via a converted school bus) it was time to do it right.

> *"You know, there's something amazing about state lines. You might think of them as meaningless political boundaries, but they often seem to demarcate physical regions as well."*

Computer system operated by handlebar keyboard, along with voice and data communications, security, and system monitoring

*Operating HF amateur radio from a field in South Carolina (1987)
Photo by Karen Greene*

Passing through Humboldt County, California in 1986. Photo by Tom Forsyth

BEHEMOTH

For nearly six years I had been wandering, collecting stories, doing interviews—frolicking in this new world where physical location was less relevant than one's choice of network providers. This was a very addicting lifestyle, and I survived by putting out a journal called *Nomadness*, selling my book, and freelance writing.

But technology was moving much faster than the ambling pace of a guy on a bicycle. I had become a spokesman for the very gizmology that was leaving me behind, stuck in the slow lane, getting whiplash from rubbernecking the miracles zipping by without having nearly enough lab time to keep up. Something had to be done; what I needed was a new machine—one with a software-defined architecture, a set of resources that could be reconfigured on the fly, a glass cockpit, more power, more communications, more file storage—more everything.

The resulting three-year project took geek bicycling to an extreme, and looking back three decades later, it's amusing to realize how much of it could have been satisfied by a modern smartphone, ham radio, and solar power system.

Weighing in at 580 pounds (fully loaded for touring), BEHEMOTH was a 105-speed beast, packed with technology from bow to stern. There was a Macintosh in the console, and in addition to the handlebar keyboard, there was a head mouse to allow cursor control while underway. A DOS machine appeared in a heads-up display below my right eye, and other workspaces appeared on dedicated LCDs behind and below the Mac. There was even a SPARCstation behind the seat, as I always wanted to ride a Unixcycle....

An on-board network allowed anything to talk to anything, and, the machine was packed with communication technology, including a huge ham radio station and a satellite earth station for electronic mail via the Internet—in 1990. And there was technology to compensate for the weight of all the technology; there were pneumatically controlled landing gear that could be deployed to give me stability when climbing a steep hill in the ultra-granny gear.

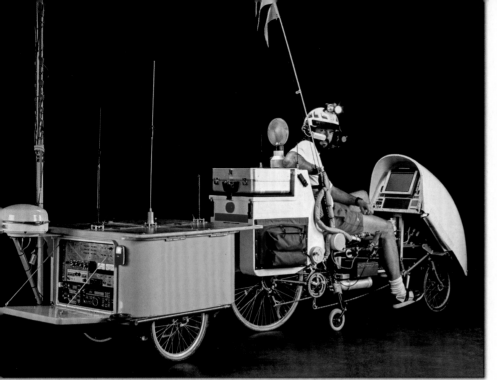

The 580-pound (fully loaded) computerized recumbent bicycle in 1992

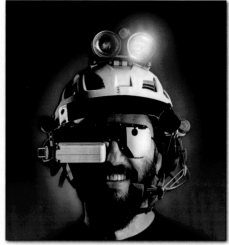

"Brain Interface Unit" was built on a Bell Tourlite bicycle helmet, and included a heads-up display, ultrasonic sensors for cursor control, a police-motorcycle comm system, stereo headphones, lights, and a liquid cooling system to reduce body temperature. Photo by Mel Lindstrom

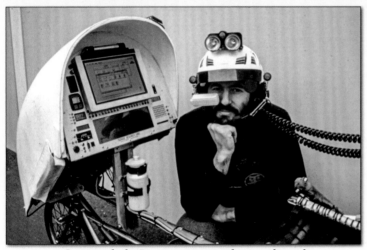

Steve with the BEHEMOTH console near the end of the project in 1991. Photo by Maggie Victor

"The most effective way to lower the quality of travel is to go somewhere. 'Going to the lake' is a functional process, with the road an obstacle lying in the way. 'Going out for a ride' is an entirely different experience—even if you take the same route and end up at the lake. People touring on bicycles usually discover this before they burn out, quickly learning to keep their goals loosely stated and in the background. It's the only way to enjoy the road: if you're just trying to 'get somewhere,' it's much more sensible to take the bus."

Sponsors and media loved it as I ambled through the midwest and up around Lake Michigan, though I was getting a little tired of the road. Soon, I was fantasizing about nautical geekery—moving all the same ideas to water. By 1992, BEHEMOTH ended up on a speaking tour as I focused on the Microship project, and in 2000, the bike moved to its new permanent home in the Computer History Museum.

 www.microship.com

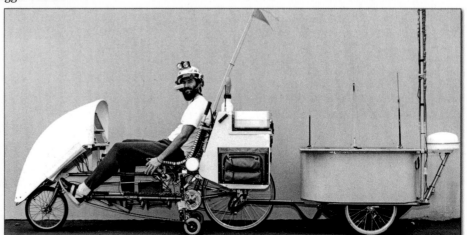

Outside the Bikelab at Sun Microsystems, which hosted the BEHEMOTH project for almost two years. Photo by Maggie Victor

Conestoga Bicycle Camper

Paul Elkins

Paul Elkins has designed and built an amazing number of unique things: bikes, boats, shelters, campers, survival gear, and a variety of Burning Man structures and vehicles. This is just one of Paul's inventions. See: **www.elkinsdiy.com**

(Paul also turned us on to Bob Stuart; see pp. 70–73.)

–LK

AFTER MAKING A HANDFUL OF FLUTED PLASTIC SHELTERS, both stationary and mobile, I wanted to try making something a little more environmentally friendly.

The simple construction techniques and materials of benders, sweat lodges, and wigwams appealed to me.

The rolling platform on this camper consists of screwed together one-by-twos and ¼-inch wood paneling for the floor. A foot hatch was added for sitting comfortably at the front table.

I tried finding willow branches for the frame, but instead opted to harvest young bamboo shoots from my neighbor's yard. Tight holes for the bamboo shoot ends were drilled in the floor with a step drill bit and secured against the inside of the frame with a nail.

"The simple construction techniques and materials of benders, sweat lodges, and wigwams appealed to me."

> *"I opted to harvest young bamboo shoots from my neighbor's yard."*

Zip-ties hold the shoots together, but to do it again, I would wait until the bamboo dried some before trimming the zip-tie adjustment tabs. Bamboo shrinks.

A 9×12-foot canvas dropcloth was used for the cover. I gathered and pinned the folds, sewed it up and trimmed the excess material. I used the bottom and innards of a used bed comforter for insulation.

The drawstring and PVC frame clamps make the cover removable for cleaning, or for removing and storing the insulation during the summer.

I wanted a light yet solid door that I could lean up against when inside, and that could swing upward to serve as an awning and standing table when deployed.

The little vented propane bottle heater with regulator and heavy-duty on-off valve for minuet control is still a work in progress, but at least I can see the flame when slowly heating up water or soup.

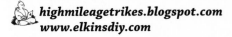
highmileagetrikes.blogspot.com
www.elkinsdiy.com

"I wanted to try making something a little more environmentally friendly."

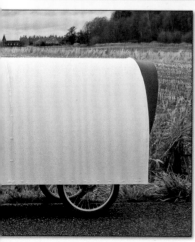

"A 9×12-foot canvas dropcloth was used for the cover."

Nomad Shepherd

Aaron Fletcher

Photos by Diane Choplin

We ran across Aaron thanks to a tip from Brendan O'Connor about this great video of him by Kirsten Dirksen of Fair Companies:
shltr.net/kirsten-aaron   *—LK*

AARON FLETCHER SAYS THAT A HALF-gallon of sheep's milk provides 2,100 calories — about enough for a person's daily recommended calorie intake. Also that sheep milk is about twice as nutritious as goat milk and almost three times as nutritious as cow milk, and — that "...the nutrition is more bioavailable for the human body to metabolize than goat or cow milk, so it often doesn't cause the allergies that some people experience with other milk."

Aaron grew up on a farm in the midwest, and migrated to the West Coast about 12 years ago. He had a small herd of miniature goats for a while, and then worked on a dairy sheep farm before branching out on his own.

For the last couple of years, Aaron has been living in a wagon and has a small herd of sheep. His home base now is on various farms in the Rogue Valley near Ashland, Oregon.

He designed the wagon, which is about six feet long and three feet wide, and had it put together by a welder. It rolls along on three BMX bike wheels. Unloaded, it weighs 150 pounds; loaded, with all his stuff, about 300 pounds.

He does farm and garden work and trades for food and places to park his wagon.

It is pulled, as you can see here, by his ram, and "I use extendable leashes to tether up to eight ewes *(female sheep)* on the non-road side, and safely guerrilla-graze them down the roadside, converting what's already growing into the most nutritious food substance."

He's passionate about sheep's milk. He drinks it and also makes cheese, yogurt, kefir, and a variety of other dairy products. When I talked to him in

"The wagon also carries the tools I need to convert the milk into cheese."

"I have about 40–50 pounds of cheese on board."

Waxed cheese kept in "cheese cave" (evaporative cooler)

February, he said, "I have about 40–50 pounds of cheese on board."

"The wagon also carries the tools I need to convert the milk into cheese, and it carries the felted wool box I made to hold the cheeses down to 60°F by simply spraying the inside down three times a day."

From the sheep's wool, he makes felt, which he fashions into clothing.

He has two solar ovens, which he uses for cooking and baking bread.

—LK

 www.123homefree.org
facebook.com/aaronfletchernomadicshepherd

"I safely guerrilla-graze them down the roadside, converting what's already growing into the most nutritious food substance."

Two baby lambs, two days old when photos were taken

FacetoFacelook
Decentralized social networking platform

name **Aaron Fletcher**

💼 | Subsistence dairy shepherd, Farmhand/sitter

🏪 | Will work/trade for local food

🕐 | Cheese making, felting wool into clothing

💬 | your health concerns, health theory, World Solutions

❤️ | interested in longterm relationship

✉️ | 541-778-7723   123Homefree.com

253

The Robo Hoboes

6,000 Miles on One-Wheelers

Dylan Weidman & Tristan Schippa

I GOT AN EMAIL FROM RICK IN LATE 2021, TELLING me that he had just seen two guys in town on electric unicycles, and he'd heard they'd come from the east coast.

It turned out that they were camping in a neighbor's yard and I was able to meet them and learn about their extraordinary trip.

Dylan and Tristan met each other in the Hudson Valley, New York in 2013. It turned out they were both interested in early prototypes of self-balancing wheels. (This is the same technology used with Segways, except these units don't have handlebars.)

Dylan says that in 2017, manufacturers started building electric unicycles that were big, capable, and fast, and he ordered one. In 2018, Tristan got a used one and started riding.

Tristan

In 2021, they both got Covid stimulus checks and bought top-of-the-line Veteran Sherman electric unicycles (about $3000 apiece), and in early September they left Germantown, New York, and headed west. They carried their gear in backpacks and stopped at coffee shops to recharge batteries.

They took the bike trail to Albany, the Erie Canal trail, made it to Buffalo, and separated for a while. When traveling separately, they followed each other on Apple maps and shared locations.

They reconnected at Lake Michigan and took a ferry across the lake (hitting a violent storm on the water). They separated again and then met up again in the Black Hills of South Dakota, traveled across Wyoming to Montana, then Highway 90, Billings, Bozeman, Butte, Missoula, eventually making it to Spokane.

"Everything was downhill after Butte," says Dylan.

From Spokane, down the east side of the Cascades, the Columbia River Gorge, Bend, Mount Shasta, and eventually into the San Francisco Bay Area. By this time, they had covered over 6,000 miles, crisscrossing across the United States.

Here they're geared up, ready to leave town for San Francisco.

"This is version 1.0. We're just getting into this lifestyle."

Dylan

Their philosophy is to be nomadic, instead of settling down. "We feel at home on the earth," says Dylan, as opposed to having a house or apartment.

Traveling so slowly, they interact closely with people and landscape. "It doesn't get more intimate," explains Dylan.

It's amazing to watch these guys ride. To demonstrate one day, Tristan took off down the road, jumping over potholes, leaning from side to side, accelerating and braking.

Dylan and Tristan were early adopters of these rigs. "This is version 1.0," says Dylan. "We're just getting into this lifestyle."

"Are there other guys doing this?," I asked Dylan.

"Not like us," he replied.

–LK

> *"They carried their gear in backpacks and stopped at coffee shops to recharge batteries."*

> It takes two hours of charging for one hour of riding, and traveling at about 25 to 30 mph, they cover about 100 miles a day. It's obviously a different way of traveling; they're getting lot closer look at countryside and people as they travel relatively short distances. And — they're not using gasoline.

On the Road in the U.S.A.

In the dead of a cold night on the Crow reservation in Montana

"Everything was downhill after Butte."

Tristan's the acrobat. Dylan says Tristan has "squirrel skills," from skiing in Vermont. This was on the bike trail crossing into Washington.

6,000 Miles to Northern California

Dylan's Tiger-cycle ready to roll out of town

Dylan's body armor

They used these hammocks throughout their trip. Here, they are set up in a World War II bunker (where the roof has been chipped open) in Northern California. They say these are high-quality hammocks and really work well.

255

Bulgarian Vardo

Cennydd Hywel Rees

Serendipity materializes at the last moment!

We've been working on this book for about a year and half now and were down to one remaining page to fill.

Flash back to 2016 when someone (anonymously) sent us a photograph of this perfect little vardo — one of those rare little structures where everything is perfect. It's a delight. Like the creations of Lloyd House or Louie Frazier, all the elements are working, and I'll say to myself, "Oh yeah!"

I posted it on my blog, asking if anyone knew where it was or who built it. No response.

Two days ago (six years later), I get an email from Bulgaria and Cen tells me that he is the mystery builder. Voila!

Here are the details from my new friend and kindred spirit in Bulgaria.

—LK

"This is one of those rare little structures where everything is perfect."

ORIGINALLY BUILT AS A PLAY SPACE for my daughter and as a guest house, my camping *karutsa* design has a long heritage and has taken both me and my family on a wonderful journey.

Karutsas, pulled by horses or donkeys, were part of a way of life now disappearing in Bulgaria.

This prototype was built from recycled materials and sleeps one to three people with comfort and style. A twist on its larger gypsy cousins, the distilled and refined design is a pure joy to be in. Once you enter, you don't want to leave.

Insulated and weather proof, you can relax comfortably inside, you can view nature, read a book, or just be.

Deceptive from the outside, the inside space is light and airy. The step-up, step-in, sit-down porch, shelves, hooks, and storage compartment provide a nautical style living system. The outside kitchen and bathroom) with tarp increase its overall usability.

This prototype has been just that. Its latest incarnation is evolving into what I hope will become a true relative of its Bulgarian cousins. A true modern hybrid, yet sympathetic to its origins and ethos.

They say form follows function — these wagons are like the Canadian canoe: just about impossible to improve upon, yet the design can be tweaked.

As we move into this new sustainable era, I hope to see my new lightweight designs again traveling the Balkans. A rolling, tiny home, fit for purpose, fit for use.

I owe a great deal to you, your work, and passions, Lloyd, and may it long continue; your books now give just as much pleasure to my children as they still do to me. I can't count the number of people I have lent them to here in Bulgaria — a constant volley of wow and *wowwwwww* every time.

Thanks again, Lloyd — the biggest hugs from us all in Bulgaria. You are welcome here any time...

About the Author's Road Rigs

My 1983 Toyota 4×4 single-cab truck on a beach in Baja California Sur about 20 years ago. Air Camping tent (made in Italy) folds up for travel, a great place to sleep up off the ground, catching breezes; no worries about scorpions or snakes in desert camping. A 12´×14´ flea market tarp with one-inch electrical conduit framework and aluminized tarp held down by ball bungees; cheap, portable shade for camping in hot climates. Corner posts held down by hanging canvas bags filled with sand. It all folds up and fits into the rooftop Yakima Rocket Box. Tent opening faces surf break.

I STARTED WITH A 1960 VW VAN IN the '60s. Bed, couch, table, fridge, closet, all in plywood. Doors swung open on side. 40 hp. Drove to Puerto Vallarta in 1964 before the bridge, where a guy walked in front to show us how to get across the river. Drove cross-country to NYC in winter, 1965, clad in sleeping bags to keep warm. I hauled half of the materials for a house I built in Big Sur on the roof rack.

Next I had a Ford pickup with a camper shell, then a Datsun 2×2 pickup. In 1988 I got my first 4×4 Toyota Tacoma, and I'm now on my third, a 2003 XtraCab 4×4, four-cylinder stick shift with a Tradesman camper shell and an aluminum Hauler rack. The famously reliable 22R motor.

My first vehicle in Baja was this little white Volkswagen "Baja bug." It was called a "pre-runner," meaning it was used to scout out the route of the Baja 1000, an annual road race between Tijuana and Cabo San Lucas. Fenders and hood were fiberglass, a 15-gallon gas tank behind the rear seat, shocks that came up and tied into the roll bars, which were just under the roof. Solar panel on roof charged two heavy-duty batteries. A great car for Baja until it ended up completely underwater in a flood.

I'm getting ready for my first Baja road trip in many years — as soon as I finish this book!

I've refurbished the tent and presently am figuring out how to mount it and at the same time carry my Yakima Rocket Box and a 10-foot surfboard on top. You can check out the trip on my blog *lloydkahn.com*; do a search for *Baja*.

My current 2003 Tacoma 4×4 with 150,000 miles. (Good for at least another 150!)

Credits

Editor and Layout: Lloyd Kahn
InDesign Layout and Photoshop: Rick Gordon
Contributing Editors: Evan Kahn, Lew Lewandowski, Lesley Kahn
Proofreader: Susan Friedland
Office Manager: Shari Dell
Printing Consultant: Trevor Shih

Line drawings by Nick Weismiller
Photo of Lloyd on title page by Aubrey Trinnaman

Printer: Hong Kong YUTO Printing Co., Ltd.
Text Paper: Golden Sun 115gsm Matt Art Paper
Cover Paper: Golden Sun 250gsm C1S Art Card

Production Hardware: Apple Macs,
   NEC LCD3090WQXi wide-gamut monitor,
   Epson Stylus Pro 4900 12-color inkjet printer

Production Software: Adobe InDesign, Adobe Photoshop, Nisus Writer Pro, BBEdit, AppleScript

Our 1973 Classic on Building

"An embarassment of riches." —*Manas*

"A piece of environmental drama" —*Building Design*

Shelter
Edited by Lloyd Kahn

$29.95   11″ × 14½″   176 pages
ISBN: 978-0-936070-11-7

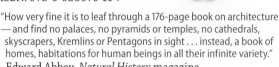

250,000 COPIES IN PRINT

"How very fine it is to leaf through a 176-page book on architecture —and find no palaces, no pyramids or temples, no cathedrals, skyscrapers, Kremlins or Pentagons in sight . . . instead, a book of homes, habitations for human beings in all their infinite variety." —Edward Abbey, *Natural History* magazine

WITH OVER 1,000 PHOTOGRAPHS, S*HELTER* is a classic celebrating the imagination, resourcefulness, and exuberance of human habitat.

First published in 1973, it is not only a record of the countercultural builders of the '60s, but also of buildings all over the world.

- It includes a history of shelter and the evolution of building types: tents, yurts, timber buildings, barns, small homes, domes, etc.
- There is a section on building materials, including heavy timber construction and stud framing, as well as stone, straw bale construction, adobe, plaster, and bamboo.
- There are interviews with builders and tips on recycled materials and wrecking.
- The emphasis is on creating your own shelter (or space) with your own hands.
- A joyful, inspiring book

The Sequel to *Shelter*

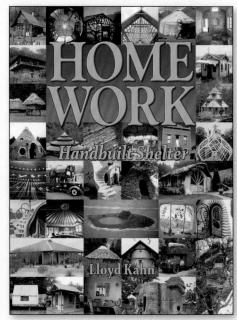

"The book is delicious, soulful, elating, inspiring, courageous, compassionate . . ."
—Peter Nabokov, Chair, Dept. of World Arts and Cultures, UCLA

"*Home Work* is a KNOCKOUT."
—John van der Zee, author of *Agony in the Garden*

Home Work
Handbuilt Shelter
by Lloyd Kahn

$32.95
9″ × 12″
256 pages
ISBN: 978-0-936070-33-9

50,000 COPIES IN PRINT

HOME WORK IS LLOYD KAHN'S SEQUEL to *Shelter* and illustrates new and even more imaginative ways to put a roof over one's head, some of which were inspired by *Shelter* itself.

- What *Shelter* was to '60s counterculture, *Home Work* is to the green building revolution.
- From yurts to caves to tree houses to tents, thatched houses, nomadic homes, and riverboats, each handbuilt dwelling blends in with its environment, using natural materials.
- 1,000 photos and 300 line drawings
- Stories of real people building and living in their own homes, plus Kahn's observations gathered over the 30 years since *Shelter* was first published

" . . . a kaleidoscopic portrait of human ingenuity"
—*San Francisco Chronicle*

Scaling Back in the 21st Century

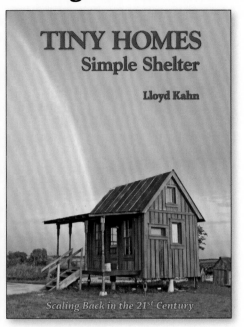

"…A glorious portfolio…"
–Penelope Green, *New York Times*

"…A genuine hit…"
–Jeffrey Trachtenberg, *Wall Street Journal*

"Gives me chills, it's so inspiring."
–Cheryl Long, Editor, *The Mother Earth News*

Tiny Homes

Simple Shelter
by Lloyd Kahn

$28.95   9″ × 12″
224 pages, 1,300 images
ISBN: 978-0-936070-52-0

75,000 COPIES IN PRINT

THERE'S A GRASSROOTS MOVEMENT IN tiny homes these days. The extremely high prices of homes, high rents, people burning out on 12-hour workdays have many people rethinking their ideas about shelter — seeking an alternative to high rents, or a lifelong mortgage debt to a bank on an overpriced home.

- Homes under 500 sq. ft.
- 150 builders
- Homes on land, on wheels, on water, even homes in the trees
- 1,300 photos, showing a rich variety of small homemade shelters
- Builders, designers, architects (no less), dreamers, artists, road gypsies, and water dwellers who've achieved a measure of freedom and independence by taking shelter into their own hands.

30% OFF ON 2 OR MORE BOOKS
Free shipping in the US

Nomadic Homes

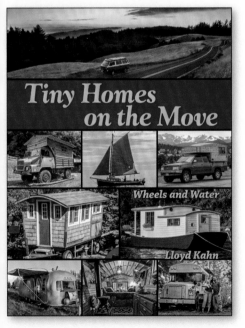

"Take an inspiring tour of the world with modern travelers who live in vans, trucks, buses, trailers, and boats that combine the comforts of home with the convenience of being able to pick up and go."
–*San Francisco Chronicle*

"A rich adventure account of nomadic lives, which will appeal to homeowners and travel fans alike."
–*The Midwest Book Review*

Tiny Homes on the Move

Wheels and Water
by Lloyd Kahn

$32.95
9″ × 12″
224 pages
ISBN: 978-0-936070-62-9

THESE HOMES MOVE! THERE ARE SOME 90 tiny homes here, either rolling on the road or floating in the water. About half of them are lived in full-time; the other half are used part-time, for trips of varying lengths upon life's highways and waterways. This book follows our best-selling book *Tiny Homes: Simple Shelter* and describes nomadic life in the 21st century.

- In the *Wheels* category are vans, pickup trucks with camper shells, house trucks, school buses, trailers, and cycles.
- In the *Water* section are sailboats and houseboats.
- There are some 1,100 color photos here, along with descriptions of each and every home.
- This is a book full of joy, adventure, and high spirits. It is rich, colorful, and imaginative, and these competent and artistic owners/builders will inspire others with their unique homes and lives.

Architecture Book of the Year

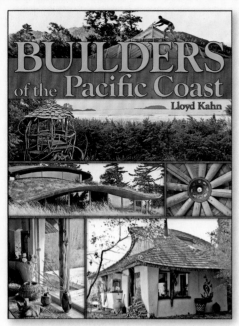

Builders of the Pacific Coast
by Lloyd Kahn

$32.95   9″×12″
256 pages, 1,200 images
ISBN: 978-0-936070-43-8

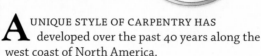

A UNIQUE STYLE OF CARPENTRY HAS developed over the past 40 years along the west coast of North America.

Here are photos of unique and creative homes from Northern Califirnia up the coast to Vancouver Island, BC.

There are three featured builders:

- Lloyd House, master craftsman and designer who has created a series of unique homes on a small island
- Bruno Atkey, builder of houses and lodges of hand-split cedar on the "Wild Coast" of Vancouver Island
- SunRay Kelley, and his wildly imaginative structures in Washington and California
- In addition, there are sculptural buildings of driftwood, homes that are beautiful as well as practical, live-aboard boats, and stunning architectural design.

"On every page is something shocking and delightful. A boat with legs. A roof like a leaf. A caravan with eyes. A split-cedar woodshed shaped like a bird. Stair rails so sinuous and snakey they might come to life and grab you. Sculpted earth walls. Round windows and arched doors. Roofs curved like seagull wings…."
–Mike Litchfield, *West Marin Citizen*

Purchase direct from:
www.shelterpub.com

Not Too Big, Not Too Small

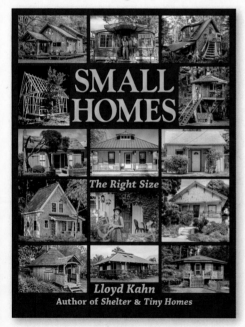

Small Homes
The Right Size
by Lloyd Kahn

$28.95   9″×12″   232 pages   1,100 images
ISBN: 978-0-936070-68-2

A RE TINY HOMES TOO SMALL FOR YOU? The average American home is 2,500 sq. ft. A typical tiny home averages 200–300 sq. ft. These small homes are 400–1200 sq. ft. — the middle ground — not too big, not too small.

- Small homes are less expensive than the average American home, use less resources, are more efficient to heat and cool, and cheaper to maintain and repair.
- Here is a way to avoid a bank mortgage or high rents, yet have more room than a tiny house affords.
- There are inspiring examples of design, carpentry, craftsmanship, imagination, creativity, and homemaking.
- Some are built with "natural materials," such as cob or straw, some with recycled wood, and some are old homes that have been remodeled. Many are in the country, some in small towns, and some in large cities.

"Small is smart. Small is beautiful."
–Kevin Kelly, *Cool Tools*

Lloyd and Lesley's Own Home

The Half-Acre Homestead
46 Years of Bulding and Gardening
by Lloyd Kahn and Lesley Creed

$19.95   8½″ × 8½″   168 pages
ISBN: 978-0-936070-81-0

Tʜɪs ɪs ᴛʜᴇ sᴛᴏʀʏ ᴏꜰ Lʟᴏʏᴅ ᴀɴᴅ Lᴇsʟᴇʏ building a home and establishing a garden on a small piece of land on the Northern California Coast over a 46-year period.

Starting with a vacant half-acre piece of land, they built their own home, created a garden with vegetables and fruit trees, and describe raising chickens, bees, and goats. The book also covers cooking, foraging, fishing, crafts, birds, and butterflies.

They have never paid rent nor have they ever had a mortgage. There are over 500 photos illustrating the above, along with:

- Maintaining a septic system
- Building greenhouses and raised vegetable beds
- Unique kitchen tools
- Advice on useful tools used in construction
- Lloyd's "if I had it to do over again" advice for building a new house

"My favorite book of yours"
–Kevin Kelly, Founder, Cool Tools (*kk.org*)

"Lloyd Kahn is 'the king of D.I.Y. dwellings.'"
–Penelope Green, *New York Times*

LIFETIME MONEY-BACK GUARANTEE ON OUR BOOKS
If you are in any way dissatisfied, call us, and we will reimburse you for the cost of the book plus postage. No need to return the book.

Building a Stud-Frame House

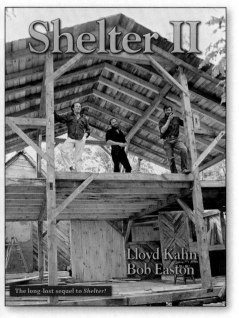

The long-lost sequel to *Shelter!*

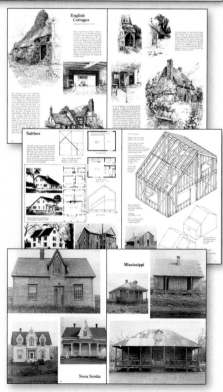

Shelter II
Edited by Lloyd Kahn & Bob Eston

$24.95   8″ × 10½″   224 pages
ISBN: 978-0-936070-49-0

Sʜᴇʟᴛᴇʀ II ᴡᴀs ᴘᴜʙʟɪsʜᴇᴅ ɪɴ 1978, five years after our book *Shelter*. A practical book for an owner-builder interested in building a simple stud-frame house. Contains a condensed 24-page instruction manual for the novice builder for building a stud-frame home:

- Climate, site, and planning
- Foundation, floor, wall, and roof framing
- Roofing, windows, doors, interior finish
- Plumbing and electrical work
- It also contains architectural drawings of five complete small homes.

"A goldmine of information about houses, house-building, and house rehabilitation ..."
–Camilla Snyder, *Los Angeles Herald-Examiner*

"From the primitive, such as a shepherd's lean-to of reeds to the ultramodern — with everything in between, including domes, barns, houseboats, adobes, tents, and log cabins; they all are here, beautifully illustrated ..."
–George Hoffmann, *Marin Independent Journal*

Building with Natural Materials

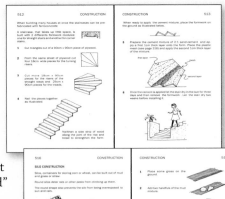

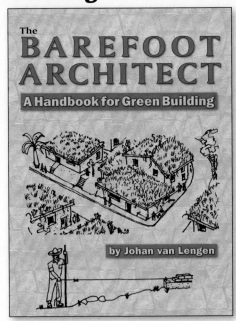

The Barefoot Architect

A Handbook for Green Building
by Johan van Lengen

$26.95 5½″ × 8½″ 720 pages
ISBN: 978-0-936070-42-1

THIS BOOK ON BUILDING WITH NATURAL materials is the first English translation of an international best-selling construction manual. It is especially oriented to building in "underdeveloped" countries. It covers:

- Basic design, site planning, and climatic considerations
- Heating, cooling, water supply
- Treating waste, and irrigation for agriculture
- Simple, basic materials — including adobe, plaster, rammed earth, wood, reinforced concrete, ferro-cement, cactus, and bamboo
- Homemade water-generated electricity, solar water heaters, wood stoves, water pumps, water distillers, and cisterns
- Septic tanks, outhouses, sand filters, and composting toilets

The World's Most Complete Guide to Septic Systems

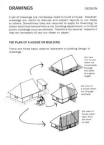

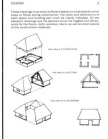

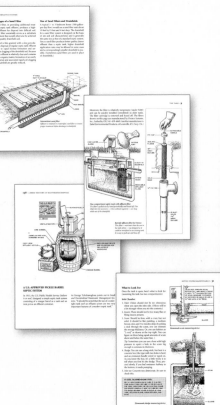

Septic System Owner's Manual

Revised Edition
by Lloyd Kahn

$22.95 8½″ × 11″ 192 pages
ISBN: 978-0-936070-40-7

OUR HANDBOOK AND GUIDE TO THE BASICS of septic systems. The book covers, in addition to septic tanks and drainfields, septic system maintenance, what to do if things go wrong, and advanced systems such as shallow drainfields, effluent filters, and trickling bio-filters — with chapters on graywater systems, composting toilets, and a unique history of water-borne waste disposal.

This is the only comprehensive, non-technical book on septic systems available for homeowners. Peter Aschwanden, illustrator of the classic *How to Keep Your Volkswagen Alive*, did the informative and witty drawings.

Shelter's Book for Children

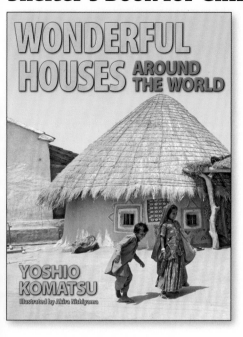

Wonderful Houses Around the World
by Yoshio Komatsu

$12.95   7½″ × 10″   48 pages
ISBN: 978-0-936070-34-6

FASCINATING AND UNIQUE, *Wonderful Houses Around the World* gives children a welcome entrée into other places and other lives throughout the world.

Two-page photographic spreads capture families outside their homes, be they simple or imposing. Detailed cutaway illustrations reveal the inside of each house, showing the various family members, especially children, engaged in typical daily activities.

Captions explain where each house is located, the environmental conditions that affect the house design, how the family lives in the home, and their possessions — all providing interesting glimpses of life in other cultures.

This book increases children's wonder about — and cultural awareness of — the many different people and ways of life around the world.

Driftwood Architecture

Driftwood Shacks
Anonymous Architecture
Along the California Coast
by Lloyd Kahn

$19.95   8½″ × 8½″   160 pages
ISBN: 978-0-936070-80-3

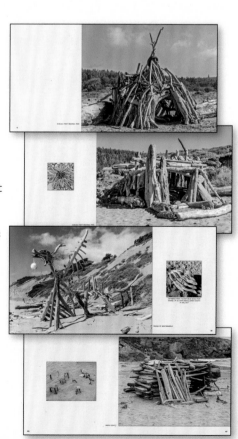

LOYD KAHN HAS BEEN HIKING AND CAMPING on Northern California beaches for the last dozen or so years and, given his background in publishing books on building, it's only natural that he would notice the unique and whimsical beach shacks constructed by anonymous builders.

Here are some 60 structures, shaped by materials lying on the beach, and ephemeral in the sense that they are built without nails, and don't last long — victims of wind, waves, and high tides.

There are also photos of beach sculptures, seaweed, seashells, birds, sea lions, whalebones, waves, surfers, fishermen, and sunsets, as well as photos from a three-day backpacking trip along the remote "Lost Coast."

A book for beachcombers and beach lovers everywhere, all of whom share a deep love for the ocean and its surroundings.

Drawing by David Wills

About the Author, About Shelter Publications

THIS IS MY 51ST YEAR PUBLISHING books. I started out working for Stewart Brand as the shelter editor of the *Whole Earth Catalog* in the late '60s and learned enough about publishing to produce two books on dome building in 1970 and 1971.

By the time *Domebook 2* sold 160,000 copies, I had figured out that domes did not work as homes. So in 1973, Bob Easton and I produced the book *Shelter*, an oversized compendium of builders and buildings around the world; it also documented the countercultural homebuilding of the '60s. The book became a hit and to date has sold over 250,000 copies and been translated into six languages.

We followed up with *Shelter II* in 1978. Then for 20 years, I published fitness books, among them, *Stretching* by Bob Anderson, *Galloway's Book on Running* by Jeff Galloway, and *Getting Stronger: Weight Training for Men and Women* by Bill Pearl.

In 2004 I got back into publishing books on building, starting with *Home Work: Handbuilt Shelter*. Since then we have published about a dozen books on building, some of which you can see in the previous six pages.

Social Media

In 2005, I started a blog — *lloydkahn.com* — and to date have put up about 5,500 posts. It's something I love doing — I've been a communicator all my life — I put a lot of time into it and for a while had a pretty big audience.

As time went by, I couldn't afford the time to keep posting at that level and, as well, Instagram came along.

I'm still doing both of these things, but in a more limited way. I'll get back into blogging as soon as I finish this book. I find the world an extraordinary place and love telling people what I discover out there.

What's Next?

Live from California

I decided to write a book on the '60s because, as a native San Franciscan who went to high school in the Haight-Ashbury district, my take on those years is way different from what I read in all the books on the era. (I have about 40 of them.)

You can see a rough draft of early chapters on my blog by clicking on **The '60s** button at the top.

Deep in the Heart of Baja

I spent 12 years traveling in Baja California — exploring, surfing, camping, and with three very close Mexican friends, getting to know the culture, customs, and history of Baja.

Barns

I've been shooting photos of barns for over 60 years now — they are my cathedrals — and I have collected about 50 books on barns. This will be a book for barn lovers.

Stay in Touch

To keep abreast of what we are doing:
Lloyd's Blog: **www.lloydkahn.com**
instagram.com/lloyd.kahn
instagram.com/shelterpub
twitter.com/lloydkahn
Shelter's Website: **www.shelterpub.com**

Rolling Homes, Volume 2

We ended up with more material than we could fit here. If you have any information about rolling homes we can share in a future book or on social media, please contact us at *shelter@shelterpub.com*.

Shelter is more than a roof overhead.